BETSY LEE

*E*xperiencing the Bright Gift of God's

Transforming Love through

Prayer

THE HEALING MOMENT

THOMAS NELSON PUBLISHERS
Nashville • Atlanta • London • Vancouver

Published in Nashville, Tennessee, by Thomas Nelson, Inc.

Unless otherwise noted scripture quotations are from THE NEW KING JAMES VERSION. Copyright © 1979, 1980, 1982, Thomas Nelson, Inc., Publishers.

Scripture quotations noted NIV are taken from the HOLY BIBLE, NEW INTERNATIONAL VERSION®. Copyright © 1973, 1978, 1984 by International Bible Society. Used by permission of Zondervan Bible Publishing House. All rights reserved.

The "NIV" and "New International Version" trademarks are registered in the United States Patent and Trademark Office by International Bible Society. Use of either trademark requires the permission of International Bible Society.

Scripture quotations noted TLB are from *The Living Bible* (Wheaton, IL: Tyndale House Publishers, 1971) and are used by permission.

Scripture quotations noted RSV are from the REVISED STANDARD VERSION of the Bible. Copyright © 1946, 1952, 1971, 1973 by the Division of Christian Education of the National Council of the Churches of Christ in the U.S.A. Used by permission.

Library of Congress Cataloging-in-Publication Data

Lee, Betsy, 1949–
    The healing moment / Betsy Lee
        p.   cm.
    Includes biographical references.
    ISBN 0-7852-8086-3
    1. Spiritual healing.   2. Spiritual life—Christianity.
I. Title
BT732.5.L36   1994
234'.13—dc20   94-12888
                                                                     CIP

Printed in the United States of America
2 3 4 5 6 7 — 99 98 97 96 95

♥

To Mary Anne Voelkel, friend and mentor,
who taught me the joy of doing
the gentle work of Jesus:
. . . lifting up those who are bowed down,
. . . helping the blind to see,
. . . setting prisoners free.

ACKNOWLEDGMENTS

❧

*T*his book was bathed in prayer. Twelve people have been praying since its inception and many more have carried it in prayer as it has progressed. To each and every one of those intercessors I am deeply grateful.

One of my own heartfelt prayers has been that I would find someone to help me "love this book into being." That prayer was answered many times over. Again and again at just the right time in the writing process, someone was sent to offer encouragement, discernment and editorial skill to help shape and sharpen the text. Special thanks go to my editors at Thomas Nelson, Lonnie Hull Dupont and Beth Clark, and additional editorial friends Roland Seboldt and Jane Campbell.

Also I would like to acknowledge the faith communities that provided "holy ground" where my prayer and healing gifts were encouraged to take root and grow: Knox Presbyterian Church in Minneapolis and Colonial Church of Edina, both in Minnesota, and the national organization of InterVarsity Christian Fellowship.

Finally, I would like to thank those who share their stories in these pages. Their stories echo the words of Rabindranath Tagore, "When I stand before thee at the day's end, thou shalt see my scars and know that I had my wounds and also my healing."

Our loving heavenly Father truly can restore the years the locusts have eaten (Joel 2:25).

CONTENTS

INTRODUCTION

❧

*T*his book is an invitation to enter fully into God's presence for a moment. To bring your burdens, hurts, doubts, fears, insecurities—all that you are—to One who loves you and longs to meet your every need.

Most of us are broken in some way and need healing. Many of us are tired and need refreshment. We face fears alone, nurse inner wounds that sap our strength, and cope with losses that weigh heavily on us. We grow apathetic, resentful, sometimes bitter.

In the midst of this, an invitation is offered. *Behold, I stand at the door and knock*, says Jesus. *Let me come into your life at a point of pain, of brokenness, of seeking and reveal My love to you, a love that can heal, comfort and renew. A love that can give you a new beginning. In Me you are a new creation* (see 2 Corinthians 5:17).

How is the door opened? By faith. It is not a big, flashy event. When we think of spiritual healing, we often think of packed auditoriums and the dramatic, booming voice of a faith healer, but that is not what this book is about. The healing moment is a quiet, personal small-scale interchange that can happen between God and you as a Spirit-filled believer. Anytime. Anywhere. And it can happen as you reach out as a channel of God's love to help someone else.

I have chosen to call this intimate interchange the "healing moment" to emphasize its accessibility to each and every Christian. As Richard Foster writes, "One of the greatest hindrances today to the free exercise of the healing ministry is the tendency to view certain aspects of it as some sort of 'big deal.'"[1] This, he says, is in direct opposition to the way of Christ.

Jesus emphasized again and again the potency of God's power released in little things. "If you have faith as small as a mustard seed," He said, "you can say to this mountain, 'Move from here to there' and it will move" (Matthew 17:20 NIV). In another instance, He likened the message of salvation to a tiny seed that can change a life if planted in a fertile heart.

So it is with the healing moment, another of God's mysteries that comes wrapped in a tiny package. Our problems often appear to loom so large, we feel paralyzed to do anything about them. We forget the seed of faith: the small moment of surrender, of trust. God challenges us to partner with Him. "Give me the little faith you *do* have and I will move the mountain." What can happen in a moment? Everything . . . if God is in it.

The healing moment is a moment of heightened awareness that allows God to touch our ordinary lives and do something extraordinary. The actual event may not last long, perhaps only a few brief minutes in prayer, but it can have far-reaching significance: a flash of insight may allow you to see the truth about yourself or a situation for the first time; you may experience God's love in a way you've never experienced before; or you may be empowered to change your life in some way.

God moves mountains in ways mysterious to us. Complete and instant healing is very rare; more often it unfolds as a process. Moment by moment, one part of a deep hurt is resolved at a time. There is a reason for this. The Lord's intent is not only to make us healed people, but whole people: fully healthy emotionally, physically and spiritually. We may come to Him complaining of an ulcer only to find that our way of relating to people emotionally is unhealthy or that the spiritual bondage of unforgiveness has a strangle hold on us physically.

Beyond that, God uses the healing process to draw us to Himself: into abiding communion, a love relationship. As He satisfies our hunger for healing, He creates in us a desire to hunger after Him. He bids us, like a lover, to taste and see His goodness, His compassion, the sheer joy of His presence.

The essence of the healing moment is being present to God and His power to heal. I invite you to explore with me how that transforming power can be released in your life to bring healing to you and those you love.

A BRIGHT GIFT

A gift opens the way for the giver and ushers him into the presence of the great.

—*Proverbs* 18:16 (*NIV*)

*A*nne rolled her racquet in her hand and bounced lightly on her toes, waiting for the serve. She felt good: really fit at fifty. Her life was full, busy, predictable. Today was Wednesday, her weekly tennis game with Marj. She looked at her partner across the net as she tossed up the ball. Anne knew that Marj's second serve would land shorter than the first and a bit to the inside. Anne stepped inside the base line ready to make a fast deep return.

Swish. Just as the ball flew by, Anne turned her head, distracted by the sound of her name. "Anne Meier," someone called at the edge of the court. "You're wanted on the phone."

Anne's racquet stopped still in her hand. Behind her, the ball hit the backdrop with a dull thud, unreturned.

"Who could that be?" Anne thought, a bit perturbed. She

waved to Marj and said she'd be back in a minute. When she picked up the phone, she heard the familiar voice of a friend, sobbing and sobbing. "Go home, Anne. Go home right away." Anne was startled. There was no further explanation. She could tell by the sound of her friend's voice that something was terribly wrong. But what? She called home and her daughter answered. She asked what had happened.

Sara said, "Just come home, Mom."

Fear gripped Anne's stomach. She wanted to know what had happened. "Is it your Dad?"

"No, Mom."

Anne insisted that Sara tell her over the phone.

"It's Danny. He's been killed."

In an instant it seemed, Anne's comfortable, predictable life was shattered. When she got home that day, she would learn that her twenty-six-year-old son, an auto mechanic, had been killed in an explosion while working on a truck. She had no way of knowing then that this sudden, unexpected tragedy would send her seeking on a long painful journey that would fundamentally transform who she was and lead to a greater wholeness than she had ever known.

♥

There wasn't time to grapple with the grief at first. Anne kept her pain inside and concentrated on what had to be done. Somehow she had to hold herself together. Funeral arrangements had to be made, notes had to be written to friends, endless details had to be taken care of.

"My grief journey really didn't begin until the day after the funeral service," said Anne, recalling her son's death three years later. Everyone had left town. The house was empty. Weary from shouldering the pain alone, Anne collapsed in a living room chair and gazed out the picture window. "The tears just poured and poured. My husband is outgoing and was able to share his grief openly, but I'm a very private person and couldn't share my feelings. I felt so vulnerable, afraid that people might say something that would crush me or try to 'fix' me—not have the patience just to sit with me in my pain. There was no other choice than to turn to God. He had always been a good listener. I was usually able to talk to Him in prayer, but, on that day, there was nothing left to tell. I just sat in silence."

As Anne sat in silence, opening herself to God, something happened. "I felt a wonderful, loving presence," said Anne. "Later, I realized it was the Holy Spirit. The Comforter. I had a sense of being held as a loving parent holds a hurting child, soothing, rocking, reassuring. The pain wasn't gone. There was still turmoil inside, but being surrounded by that Love, so tender and embracing, made the pain bearable.

"It was as if a river of love flowed out to me, through me and out to the rest of the world." That river of love even seemed to flow between Anne and her son. Instead of feeling bereft and abandoned by his death, Anne felt surprisingly close to him in that moment—a different kind of closeness than when he was alive.

"My relationship with Danny had been so encumbered with little fears, guilt, unfair expectations. He had been a difficult child to raise. He was hyperactive, learning disabled. He got into a great deal of trouble. As he grew older, the discouragement he felt living in a performance-oriented family and competitive school system led to alcoholism. We spent time working through chemical dependency counseling; he was able to maintain sobriety, but it was a hard road.

"Now those things didn't matter anymore," Anne said. "The

barriers were gone. I had a sense that it was a healing for Danny as well as for me. I knew he was rejoicing because now he could love his family and friends freely as he always wanted to."

What Anne experienced in her living room that day was a healing moment—the beginning of a journey that would lead to healing in all aspects of her life. It was mysterious, something she couldn't understand. Something wonderful. She came to think of it as a "bright gift."

As she felt the gift of unconditional love flowing freely between her and her son, she also experienced a healing in her own heart. "A big part of the healing was feeling forgiven, becoming more compassionate toward myself. Every parent takes responsibility for the death of a child. There is remorse, guilt. Constant flashbacks of mistakes and failures. The mistakes were so painful to look at. I could never think of being forgiven. Yet when the pain surfaced, I felt that river of love washing over me, a great sense of being forgiven as if the past was erased, forgotten."

❧

Every time Anne relived the healing moment she experienced in her living room, it touched her more deeply and it began to work a lasting change in her. "I felt surrounded by God's love, by His 'lovingkindness and tender mercies' as Psalm 103 says. I began to know, really know, for the first time in my life that God loved and cherished me.

"A funny thing happened," said Anne. "Things that used to make me feel inadequate, little human failings, didn't matter anymore because I was so aware of how much God loved me. As I became more compassionate toward myself, I became more compassionate toward other people. Less manipulative and judging.

"God took the healing of my grief into the rest of my life and healed much, much more than I could have imagined."

Anne's relationship with God became deeper and richer. She spent more time in listening prayer. Gradually, even her workaholism and drivenness began to disappear. "When my son died, a friend had suggested that I quit work to take care of my grief. That seemed out of the question at the time. I had just lost my identity as Danny's mother, now she was asking me to give up my successful, hard-working identity too. But eventually I came to realize that my true self wasn't happy just working for money. I wanted to become the person God made me."

Several years later Anne did decide to take her friend's advice and leave her sales job. She took time to slow down and discover new aspects of herself. Anne's bright gift of healing is still being opened, bringing new joys and fulfillment—to herself and to others.

Instead of letting grief paralyze her, Anne's healing gave her the freedom to move on by exploring ways to celebrate her son's short life. "Every day I pray for God to make me a kinder person in [Danny's] memory." Anne is known in her neighborhood, her church, the community as one who comforts others. One of her greatest joys now is reading aloud to residents at a nursing home. Anne developed this ministry in memory of Danny because he was never able to read well and because as a child he loved hearing his mom read to him. There are times, Anne says, when her listeners, many in their nineties with strokes and Alzheimer's, are moved by what she reads. "Tears come to their eyes and they are embarrassed. I tell them not to be ashamed. Tears are God's healing."

It was through tears that Anne had grown: hidden tears that only God could see; hot tears that poured out of the open wound of grief; tender tears that lapped over her soul like waves, washing away self-hate, guilt, anger; and finally, tears of joy as she opened herself fully to One who loved her far more deeply than she ever could have imagined.

A GIFT OPENS THE WAY

God's healing comes in many ways. It may come serendipitously as it did for Anne, almost as an accidental discovery, or it may come after years of hard seeking. However it comes, there is always an element of grace about it that fills the receiver with awe and gratitude—not just for the gift of healing itself, as wonderful as that is, but also for the Giver of the gift.

To know God as One who hears and responds to prayer, personally, intimately—touching the core of who we are—opens up a new way of seeing and being. It is to see and experience just how vast and deep God's heart is, to begin to grasp a love "that is higher than the heavens" and "wider than the sea." To open ourselves to that grandeur lifts the human spirit and enlarges our perspective.

"I weep a lot still," wrote a friend who had just experienced this love in a healing moment. "God is so alive! His love is strong and generous. I just can't get over it really. I'm constantly in awe."

Pain paralyzes the emotions, cripples the body, imprisons the mind. Love liberates. It releases us to embrace life, health and wholeness. It flings open the door of possibility and empowers us to change.

How can this love be ours? Years ago I began to experience healing moments in my own life. They came like accidental discoveries, as Anne's did, usually when I was hurting and crying out to God. Sometimes I was consciously seeking Him in prayer; other times the longing, the ache went unspoken. It was just a feeling, a sense of my own neediness.

I was overwhelmed by God's love when He met me in these moments, overcome by how well He knew me, how accepting He was, how tender was His presence. These times of feeling the nearness of God were so incredible, they created an expectancy in me. I had a sense that God actually longed for them more than I did, that He really yearned to break through in my life. It occurred to me that if I were only more open to these momentary encounters, they would become less of a rarity, a "happening," and more integrated into my regular prayer life.

Gradually, I discovered that it *was* possible to consciously enter into these moments—not engineering them, because they would always remain a mystery, and if healing came, it would always be a gift—but opening myself more fully to God, becoming more receptive, responsive, more accustomed to hearing Him speak and seeing Him move in my life. Now these moments occur not only during my prayer times, but at any time, often when I least expect it. Sometimes, God has come gently to heal a hurt perhaps too deep for me to acknowledge, some hidden pain I wasn't even aware of. With David, I've had to wonder out loud: how do you know, God, my thoughts even before I think them, my words before I speak them (Psalm 139:2–4)!

Being aware of the healing moment has made me attentive to significant experiences which otherwise would have gone unnoticed. When I do notice them, I often carry them in my mind for a long time, pondering them as Mary did the angel's visitation, understanding a little bit more each time the treasure I've been given.

As Anne discovered, the healing moment is a gift. Thinking

of it as a gift, there is a process you can use to allow this special experience to unfold in your own life:

1. *Recognize that the gift is there.* This requires "seeing" with the eyes of faith and being present to God so He can be present to you.
2. *Receive it.* To receive a gift your hands must be open; so in prayer your heart must be open to receive the healing moment. This means letting go of distractions, self-preoccupation, expectations so that you are free to embrace what God wants to give.
3. *Open it.* Once you've received the gift, you need to open it. This requires getting actively involved in the process: it is your response to God's expression of love, your full engagement of mind, heart and will as you explore what the gift is.
4. *Use it.* Until you put a gift into use, it remains just an attractive object to admire. The healing moment is meant to be not just a moving prayer experience—which it often is—but also something practical that is worked out very concretely in your daily life.

In the following sections we'll explore these four steps in greater detail so that you can understand the process more fully.

RECOGNIZING THE GIFT

You may have read Anne's story and thought longingly how wonderful it would be to feel God's presence so close in a time of need, to experience His love so deeply, so tangibly. If only, you're thinking, that could happen to me.

It can. The first step in allowing it to happen in your own life is to understand this about the nature of God: God is a giver of good gifts. "Ask, and it will be given to you," said Jesus. "What man is there among you who, if his son asks for bread, will give him a stone? Or if he asks for a fish, will he give him a serpent? If you then, being evil, know how to give good gifts to your children, how much more will your Father who is in heaven give good things to those who ask Him" (Matthew 7:7, 9–11).

The gift-giving nature of God is lavishly woven throughout Scripture. From the very beginning in Genesis when God gives the gift of life itself, to Revelation when Jesus holds out the free gift of eternal life, God is seen as a generous giver. Jesus Himself is called an "indescribable gift" (2 Corinthians 9:15); Jesus in turn says that the Father will send the gift of the Holy Spirit after He is gone (Acts 1:5); in addition, spiritual gifts are given to empower each and every believer (Ephesians 4:7–13). God is a giver of good gifts, and there is no gift He so yearns to give as the gift of healing. "God hurts to heal," wrote C. S. Lewis. He knows our woundedness and suffers with us when a relationship with a loved one is broken, when we confront disappointment or loss, when we feel rejected.

God so loved men and women who were hurting that He sent Jesus to walk among them to demonstrate that love. "In the Gospels," writes Francis MacNutt, "you see him spending a large part of his time going from one sick person to another, laying his hands on them and healing them. His heart goes out to people."[1] Jesus touched the blind and they could see, the crippled and they could walk; He reached out his hand in forgiveness to sinners, in peace to the fearful, in affirmation to the lonely.

He not only demonstrated compassion, but because He was the Son of God, He also showed that He had the power to change things. Jesus said that the purpose of the healing miracles was to make visible the spiritual kingdom of love that He preached about. On one hand, these marvelous acts pointed to a kingdom to come—where every tear would be wiped away and death and disease defeated; on the other hand, Jesus' miracles brought this new reality into immediate human experience, into the "now."

Just as Jesus brought the kingdom of love to people by physically touching them two thousand years ago, He longs to be as real to us now as He was then. How is this possible? It is possible through the power of the Holy Spirit. The Holy Spirit, imbedded in the heart of the believer, creates a current of communication that flows between the heart of God and that part of our hearts that is responsive to Him. The Holy Spirit enables us to believe: to "see" Jesus with the eyes of faith, to feel the tenderness of His touch, to sense His very presence.

RECEIVING THE GIFT

"A man who prays," writes Henri Nouwen, "is a man standing with his hands open to the world. He knows that God will show himself in the nature which surrounds him, in the people he meets, in the situations he runs into . . . Prayer creates that openness where God can give himself to man. Indeed, God wants to give himself; he wants to surrender himself to the man he has created, he even begs to be admitted into the human heart."[2]

Most of us find Nouwen's words astounding. Often when we are hurting, we blame God for not being there when we need Him, for being distant, unconcerned, hidden—certainly not begging to be admitted to our hearts! And yet are we open to *His* overtures? When God is present to us, are we present to Him? My experience, like Nouwen's, is that God longs to reveal

Himself at every turn in our lives. He is not distant and preoccupied. We are.

One particular experience brought this home to me. During a prayer time one spring day, God seemed to draw me outside to experience Him in nature. A cedar deck wraps around our house, which is surrounded by lush, green woods. In the three years we had lived there, I had never really taken the time to notice the beauty outside my window. Standing on the deck, I took several deep breaths, filling my lungs with fresh air, drinking in the sunshine like the newly budding leaves in the woods. As I did this, I seemed able to open my heart and drink in the immensity of God's love in a way that I could not do by simply sitting at my living room table. Day by day, the woods and pond nearby became an inviting place of rest and refreshment in my busy life. Every time I spent time there, God revealed something new. One morning when I was gazing at the pond, I heard the instruction, *Circle it.*

"Circle it?" I puzzled. It was a particularly demanding day, and I didn't have time to walk around the pond. "What if I meet a neighbor along the way and have to stop to chat?" I argued with the inner voice. No, I decided, some other day. I turned to go back to the house.

Circle it, I heard the instruction again, this time more insistent.

"Why?" I asked, a little startled by the firmness of the voice. I knew it was Jesus.

Because I want to show you some things I cannot tell you any other way.

So I followed: a bit reluctantly, out of obedience. As we walked (I use the word "we" because I had a clear sense that Jesus was walking beside me like a friend), my mood changed. This was a walk unlike any other walk and soon I was filled with wonder. It was just a brief interlude of time—maybe fifteen minutes—but it was a very intimate time of sharing in which Jesus chose to reveal significant things about Himself and our relationship.

At one point I stopped to rest. I looked up and gazed across the pond to the crest of the hill where I usually stood. A gentle breeze rustled the delicate fronds of a weeping willow that arched over my head. *When you weep,* Jesus said, *I weep with you.* This was deeply moving to me because the pond was a place where I could pour out my secret pain, where I often let tears go that were bottled up inside. I thought of all the times Jesus had stood at this spot watching me, entering into my pain, helping me bear it even though I was not aware of His presence. What a profound expression of love that was.

Jesus' words were reassuring, comforting, a precious gift, for often the pain of knowing we suffer alone is a wound in itself. Hearing those words was a healing moment for me.

How easily such a moment can be missed! It would have been so easy not to have walked around the pond that day, so easy to have ignored an inner prodding to be open to the whisperings of the Spirit, so easy not to have received that gift of insight.

To receive God's gifts—often so fleeting and rare—sometimes we need to let go of crowded schedules and all the distractions which clamor for our attention. There are also deeper things that we need to relinquish in order to fully embrace what God would give. Ted Loder captures these hidden strangle holds on our lives in his poem, "Guide Me Into an Unclenched Moment"[3]:

Gentle me,
Holy One,

into an unclenched moment,
a deep breath,
a letting go
of heavy expectancies,
of shriveling anxieties,
of dead uncertainties,
that, softened by the silence,
surrounded by the light,
and open to the mystery,
I may be found by wholeness,
upheld by the unfathomable,
entranced by the simple,
and filled with the joy
that is you.

Expectations, worries, fears—these are the more elusive, pervasive blocks to spiritual openness, stubborn parts of our personalities that resist vulnerability. And yet Nouwen says that "prayer creates an openness." Prayers of confession can root out and release hidden burdens; prayers of praise can draw us upward and outward, beyond our worries, to a spacious place where we can let go of the temporal and rest in the eternal.

Prayer has a way of wearing away our hard, outer shells and making our hearts tender. Gradually, we become more and more open to the stirrings of the Spirit. In faith, we let go and lean into the unknown, ready to respond to God's overtures in our lives.

LETTING THE GIFT UNFOLD

If you remember Anne's story, Anne was aware that God was reaching out to her in her grief, and she opened herself to His healing presence. She recognized the experience as a significant moment, and she received it as a gift. But that was only the beginning. She went back to her living room and relived that moment again and again for several weeks, each time savoring something new from the experience. Beyond that, she let the specific healing moment unfold, over a period of years, into all aspects of her life. "God took the healing of my grief into the rest of my life," she said, "and healed much, much more than I could have imagined."

One friend of mine described the healing moment as a seed. By that, she meant that the experience was deeply planted in her heart and could not be completely understood immediately. It was only as she cultivated the experience, prayerfully reflecting on it and letting it release its transforming power in her life, that the full impact of the experience was truly felt.

God gives the gift, plants the seed, but the extent to which it unfolds in our lives is determined by how responsive we are. As in the parable of the sower, if our hearts are hard, the healing moment cannot take root and begin to grow at all; if our faith is shallow, the experience will only be emotional and quickly forgotten; if our spirits are thorny, skepticism will cause us to doubt the experience; but if sown in a receptive heart, the healing power of such a moment can actually be multiplied many times over.

Are there ways you can increase your responsiveness to the Spirit? Yes. I've observed that different people respond with varying degrees of openness to the healing moment; indeed even in one person's life there is a difference depending on the individual's receptivity at the time. To increase your responsiveness:

1. Be available. Set aside time for solitude and reflection to listen to God; it is most often in prayer that these moments come.

2. Soak in the Word. Being in the Word daily is the best way to learn to hear God speak and keep your heart sensitive and yielded to the Spirit.

3. Be aware of unconfessed sin, bitterness, unforgiveness. These are hindrances to the free flow of the Spirit; they shut you off from your true self and put up a barrier between you and God. Repent in prayer; express forgiveness to those you have hurt and let go of harbored resentments caused by those who have hurt you.

4. Be part of a Spirit-filled community of believers. The healing moment is a private moment, but other Christians keep you honest and vulnerable, build your faith, and provide encouragement so that you are more open to healing.

5. If you're seeking healing for a particular hurt, ask a trusted friend to intercede for you. Partnership in prayer protects you from Satanic attack and doubles the effectiveness of your own prayers (Matthew 18:19).

6. Finally, rest in the knowledge that God knows in the ripeness of time when you are ready for a healing moment. He has been preparing you for it long before it happens and He will unfold its meaning afterward. Relax. Rest in Him . . . and simply be open.

When Anne Meier described her healing moment, she had to reach for words to capture the mystery of what happened: "It was like a river of love that flowed out to me, through me and out to the rest of the world." Anne was suggesting that the experience was not merely a single event, frozen in time; but rather it was fluid, moving, part of a process. And so it is.

First, there is the in-working of the moment—receiving the healing God gives and letting it transform your life from within—and then there is the out-working, which is just as important. You may not be moved as dramatically as Anne was to change your lifestyle or to launch into ministry, but as the seed of the experience takes hold in your heart and grows, it will produce fruit for all to see.

The wonder of prayer is that this process begins with only a small moment of seeking and surrender, with a man or a woman, hungry for healing, "standing with hands open to the world."

YOUR HEALING MOMENT

Perhaps you are that man or woman, hungry for healing. I don't know where you hurt and why. God does. He knows your need and longs to meet it. He comes to each of us, asking us to reach out to Him. If we are willing to take the risk to open our hearts, believing, He promises to be present to us.

God comes to us in Jesus and Jesus comes to us in prayer. The following chapters of this book are organized thematically around different points of need, which act as doors for you to walk through and meet Jesus. You can read the book all the way through, or you may sense an urge to dip into the chapter where your greatest felt need is at the moment. Feel free to do that. It may be here that Jesus longs to touch you in immediacy and power.

At the end of each chapter you will be invited to enter into a personal prayer experience. Each prayer is centered around a Scripture scene. You are encouraged to imagine yourself in the scene: experiencing through your senses the actual sights, sounds and smells of the setting. This is more than an imaginative exercise. This kind of interactive prayer can allow you to encounter Jesus face to face, to meet *Jehovah-Shammah*, the

"God who is there," ready to heal and help, in the living pages of Scripture.

My hope is that you will not only receive healing and empowerment from these prayers—as wonderful as that will be—but that, beyond that, you will come to know Jesus as friend, companion and Lord. That you will look past the gift to the Giver, past your healing to the Healer, to the One who is always there. Tangible. Touchable. Knowable.

There is another emphasis in this book beyond knowing Jesus and receiving the gift of healing. As you receive the gift, in gratitude you'll feel that compassion flowing out to someone else. You'll become a "gifted giver." It will happen almost imperceptibly through no effort of your own. Just as pain was once part of you, now healing will become part of you. As you grow in sensitivity to the Spirit and to others, God will equip you to be part of His redemptive work in the world.

"Every human being is called upon to be a healer," writes Henri Nouwen. "We are all healers who can reach out to offer health, and we are patients in constant need of help."[4]

We reach out in the name of Jesus, in our weakness, in His strength—and miracles happen.

A young man reaches out to forgive and bless a father who has hurt him; a divorcee begins to serve others as her self-image is restored. And the gift goes on. Something of the Giver Himself is imparted in the gift He gives. The generosity, the compassion, the gift-giving nature of God.

Are you ready to receive the gift God wants to give you? As a gesture of your willingness to be open to God, put this book aside and rest your hands in your lap, palms up. Close your eyes in prayer. Ask God if there is anything—an overcrowded schedule, fixed expectations, worries, fears, mistrust—you need to relinquish in order to be fully receptive and attentive to Him.

Turn your hands over, palms down, as a gesture of letting go of these things. Feel the freedom of letting go. Then gently turn your open hands up again. Let your spirit rest in the joy of new possibilities. When you feel free to respond, offer a simple prayer of submission: "Yes, Lord, I'm ready to receive your gift of healing. I'm ready to receive You."

THE GIFT
OF ACCEPTANCE

*Those who look to him are radiant; their faces are
never covered with shame.*

—*Psalm 34:5 (NIV)*

*T*ake a few minutes to be absolutely quiet and reflect. Ask
yourself, "What is my deepest need?" Tune out the noise
of daily distractions and become fully attentive to your heart's
deepest longings. This question may make you uncomfortable.
Sometimes it is hard to confess our own neediness, but just for a
moment ask yourself, "What is my deepest need?"

Perhaps you cannot articulate the feeling. It may be a sad
feeling, a disappointing feeling, an empty feeling. Perhaps you
feel sometimes like an imposter, appearing competent and successful to your friends, but inside fearing that you can never
measure up. "The bottom line," confided a friend one time, "is
that I don't feel loved for who I am." So many of us struggle
with a deep-seated hunger for acceptance and unconditional
love. Is that your need?

I have found as the Lord heals me and as I pray with others for Jesus to mend the broken pieces of their lives, that the need for acceptance is one of the most common cries for healing. There are many reasons for this. Some of us, normally self-assured, can suddenly experience low self-worth as a result of a crippling loss: the death of a loved one, divorce, the loss of a job, a broken relationship. There are others who struggle with rejection all their lives: it may be rooted in a childhood trauma, eg. incest, abuse or abandonment; it may be from the pervasive pain inherent in a dysfunctional family system.

In this chapter, we will look at ways God heals rejection and shame. As human beings, we all suffer feelings of loss, rejection and shame—deep wounds to our personhood. These are inner wounds that other people cannot see, wounds that we often do not acknowledge ourselves. But pain is not easily circumvented, coped with, or denied. Unless it is worked through to a point of resolution and healing, it is always there. And it accumulates.

Our hearts are very tender. To realize what inner wounds can do to us, imagine your heart as a peach: fragile, crushable. Picture someone holding that peach high above a hard floor and dropping it. *Ouch!* This might be analogous to a first rejection; even in the womb, many believe a fetus can sense rejection if the pregnancy is unwanted. A few years later, a new sibling pushes you out of mother's arms. The delicate fruit is dropped again—*wince!*—leaving another bruise. Throughout your childhood, Dad, absorbed in his work, ignores your pleas for attention. *Ouch! Ouch!* More bruises. You're publicly humiliated at school. *Wince!* As a teenager, you're sexually abused. *Shhh!* You swallow the pain. An early marriage fails. *Squiiiish!* The wounds fester.

You may be able to relate to this catalog of hurts, or they

might be completely outside your experience. Rejection is a very personal thing: what one person considers an unkind slight might be devastating to someone else. And each person reacts to rejection differently. You may be one who suffers silently, driven gradually through the years to severe depression; you may try to escape the pain through busyness; or constant rejection may leave you numb and distant, unable to risk intimacy. Can the damage of a bruised and battered heart ever be repaired?

There is One who knows our pain, every bruise, every hurt—even those hurts we have never shared with those closest to us. He was sent, and still sends others by His Spirit, to "heal the brokenhearted" (Isaiah 61:1). As He mends what is broken, He is so gentle, so tender in His touch, that "he will not break a bruised reed" (Isaiah 42:3). He is One who has known suffering, known rejection, and willingly takes our pain into Himself; then, through the mystery of love, takes what cripples us and turns it into a gift.[1]

BEING DRAWN INTO GOD'S CIRCLE

Whether our hearts have been bruised by dents and mars—little hurts, disappointments, rebuffs—or pounded into fragments by a lifetime of woundedness, each of us has felt unloved and unlovely at times. We have all had the door of rejection slammed in our face. It is cold beyond the bounds of belonging; it is lonely, it is frightening. So the Shepherd comes seeking. "The world drew a circle and shut me out," someone has said, "God drew a circle and drew me in."

Perhaps as a child you remember the picture of Jesus as a shepherd carrying a little lamb on His shoulders: the one out of a flock of hundred that was lost. This is more than a sentimental picture. It is the essence of Jesus' healing ministry: to seek and to save what is lost. Perhaps as you read these words, you feel like a lost sheep. Lonely. Needy. Crippled by hurt from someone else's sin . . . or your own. Driven by anger and rebellion, you may have strayed beyond the safety of the fold: you find yourself at the bottom of a deep, dark hole—self-pity—or hanging on to the edge of a cliff, about to drop into an abyss of hatred. Rejection can lead to any of these dark situations.

How does Jesus call us back to Himself and heal our hurts? First, He calls us by name (John 10:3). The methods He uses to find us, the circumstances, the people in our lives, the ways He communicates with us are all highly individual—unique and personal to each of us. All of this, even before we receive the healing we need, is meant to express His complete acceptance and understanding of who we are.

My seven-year-old slid under her bunkbed the other day to nurse a hurt. She is too old for me to force her out of hiding and yet I knew our communication needed to be restored. She had said some things that hurt me. I cooled off, counted to ten, prayed. Then I was ready to reach out in reconciliation. I walked quietly into her room and laid on the floor next to her and waited. After a while, she stopped sobbing. She began to tell me about lots of things going on in her life that I didn't know about: rejection at school and in the neighborhood. I listened sympathetically; she soon came out from under the bed and we became friends again. That is how Jesus comes to us: He knows our hiding places. He comes to us right where we are and lovingly draws us out until He wins our trust.

Secondly, as a shepherd, Jesus guides us (John 10:4). He invites us to follow Him through the healing process—a process that is different for everyone. Again, Jesus takes great care to respect our temperaments and find a pace that is comfortable for us: forceful enough to call us forward, but gentle enough to rest us when we need it.

In this chapter, we'll look at three distinct ways Jesus heals rejection: affirmation, healing of memories, and interactive prayer. All of these are specific kinds of healing moments effective in different situations. Just as a surgeon has a range of tools, so the Great Physician uses a variety of ways to heal a broken heart.

Finally, Jesus calls us into community as He heals (John 10:16). According to *The American Heritage Dictionary*, the word *rejection* means "the refusal to accept or recognize, to discard as defective or useless, to throw away." That language is not too strong to describe what it feels like to be the rejected partner in a divorce, or a child completely ignored by workaholic parents, or to be otherwise cast out of the family circle.

I have a friend who is a social worker. She had grown accustomed to hearing painful story after painful story from a litany of broken homes. She dealt with them all pragmatically in a businesslike way until one story stopped her. In an affluent suburb, a toddler in his diapers was left intentionally in a trash can, waiting for the weekly garbage pick-up. As the mother of a toddler herself, my friend could not bear the pain of listening to one more heartwrenching story. That day she walked out of the office and never came back.

Sadly, many of our families are no longer the circle of love they once were. Through most of the 1970s and 1980s, a million children a year watched their parents split up. In too many families, parents are abdicating their shepherding roles by neglecting—even cruelly abusing—their "lambs."[2] The number of reported cases of child abuse has doubled in a decade. Experts predict that one of every four girls will be sexually abused *within the family* by age eighteen. With boys the chances are one in eight.[3]

Now, as never before, we desperately need a compassionate Shepherd who seeks and finds what is lost, discarded, abandoned, and restores each and every human being to his or her true worth.

Jesus knew the agony of abandonment. He died outside the walls of Jerusalem, cast out by His own people, deserted by His closest friends, even forsaken by His Father as He took on the sins of the world. Golgotha, the "place of the skull," was literally a garbage heap outside the city walls. Jesus knew physical abuse. Crucifixion was the most excruciating death imaginable in the Roman world at that time. He suffered a long, slow torturous death: His flesh crushed and lacerated by scourging, His hands and feet pounded through with iron spikes. Jesus was emotionally abused, spit at, and ridiculed. Finally, Jesus was sexually shamed, enduring the final humiliation of hanging naked, exposed to public view as flies from the debris around Him feasted on His open wounds.

Why such a horrible death? Why such pain? Because Jesus took the full brunt of our sin and sin is ugly, raw. The cross was Jesus' final confrontation with the evil He came to defeat. "The only ultimate way to conquer evil is to let it be smothered within a willing, living human being. When it is absorbed there like blood in a sponge or a spear into one's heart, it loses its power and goes no further."[4]

Death lost its power that day. The Good Shepherd became a lamb that He might experience our pain, and gave His life that we might know His love.

Jesus' sacrifice on the cross atoned for our sin. He broke down the "wall of hostility" that separates us from God, from others and from our true selves, making us "at one" with Him again. He willingly took the consequences of our sin upon Himself and restored the fellowship with our Creator that gives us such a deep sense of well-being and wholeness. This oneness makes it possible to reconcile all our other relationships.

God's desire is not only to heal individuals, but also to heal families, churches, communities. "Behold, how good and pleasant it is for brethren to dwell together in unity!" exclaimed the psalmist. "For there the Lord commanded the blessing—life forevermore" (Psalm 133:1, 3). We are made in God's image, made for relationship. Even though these relationships are wrought with conflict sometimes, even torn in two, God is always drawing us back into the circle of His love where they can be mended and restored.

How does He do this? One of the methods He uses is so simple and unassuming, we tend to overlook it, and yet it is available to us all.

THE HEALING POWER OF AFFIRMATION

To affirm means "to give firmness to, to strengthen, to make firm." Affirmations are specific words and actions that build a person up, that nurture the soul and foster a healthy sense of self. Without this free and loving expression of acceptance, we never feel confident, even okay, about who we are. On the other hand, expressions of genuine acceptance and caring can transform a shattered self-image and even begin to heal the worst wounds of rejection.

One Sunday morning after a morning church service, an old acquaintance threaded his way through the milling congregation to my side. He introduced himself and hesitantly asked if I remembered him. He and his wife had attended our church years ago. She was a friend of mine and I had met Dave through her.

When I told him I was glad to see him, he managed a weak smile. Even though I did remember Dave, I could hardly believe this was the same person I had known.

My mind did a quick flashback. I saw Dave relaxing on the living room floor of a warm and comfortable apartment. As he and his new wife talked about how they met, Dave looked like a kitten, young and playful, lounging on a cozy braided rug. I couldn't help but notice his Mickey Mouse socks!

The man standing in front of me several years later on that Sunday morning looked anything but young and playful. He wore a dark suit and seemed much older than he really was. His shoulders slumped and his hand trembled as I shook it. He looked wounded, emotionally frail. He seemed to be fighting back tears.

He confessed that he had been sitting in the back pew for weeks wanting to come up and talk to me, but he was afraid I wouldn't want to talk to him because I was his wife's friend and he thought I would blame him for what happened.

Then Dave told me about the divorce. He and his wife had moved across the country and we had lost contact. It came as a sad surprise to me. "She just didn't want to be married to me anymore," he shrugged his shoulders. The divorce had been devastating, leaving Dave visibly shattered.

I listened to Dave's pain, not knowing what to say. Words seemed inadequate, superficial.

I was looking into the eyes of someone who had suffered such deep rejection that he did not have an ounce of self-worth left anymore.

I found myself doing something surprising. After Dave had shaken my hand, normally I would have dropped my hand as I would with any casual acquaintance. But as Dave shared his brokenness, I found myself still holding his hand. As I did this, I felt a surge of love flowing through me to him. It was not just compassion, though I did feel that; it was something more. I sensed that Jesus wanted to touch Dave through me. I found myself radiating warmth and acceptance, not in a forced way, but rather gently, naturally, and as Dave received this acceptance, I saw his downcast eyes visibly brighten. His whole body seemed to relax.

I heard myself say with sudden boldness: "Dave, you've come to the right place. You've come to a healing place."

This whole interchange only lasted about five minutes, but something significant took place in that moment. Dave began to change. As he became involved in the life of the church, many people commented on the change they saw in him. He seemed to grow stronger and more confident right in front of our eyes. He began to think of himself as someone of value with something to give, not just a cast off to be pitied. He became a regular at our early morning prayer group. Weeks later when a hurting husband came needing prayer for a troubled marriage, Dave put his arm around the man and offered encouragement.

How can I say that this dramatic turnaround happened in Dave's life just because of our brief conversation that Sunday? Dave himself said that moment was pivotal, but also I sensed, even as the moment unfolded, that Jesus was reaching out to begin to heal Dave's shattered self-image. He was doing it through me, though I had no idea at the time it could be so profound. I simply felt His presence in the power of the moment and knew the Spirit was in it.

I was amazed that God uses so little to do so much—through a hug, a handshake, expressions of affection, words of affirmation, valuing people for who they are. "Hospitality is not to change people," writes Henri Nouwen, " but to offer them space where change can take place."[5] Such acceptance is a gift that can heal.

I am not suggesting that the hard work of truly healing deep pain can be resolved in an instant as if waving a magic wand. Dave walked away after our meeting still the victim of a devastating divorce. His marriage was not healed. His life still looked pretty tragic: he was forty and knew he might not ever have the children and the home he always dreamed of. But somehow in that healing moment he was deeply changed—some of the despair was gone, hope flooded in, and he began to take constructive steps toward restructuring his life rather than remaining forever bitter and paralyzed by the past.

What I *am* saying about the healing moment—whether we receive it or give it—is that it is hard for us to grasp how much God can do if He decides to move through such a moment.

Francis MacNutt contends that people have been healed just by the way someone looked at them. "They experienced the presence of Jesus coming through a Christian's eyes, and it was enough to heal them. Nor should this surprise us. If we can be infected with sickness by getting near sick people, why shouldn't we be touched by life and health when we draw close to the source of life, Jesus?"[6]

Drawing close to the source of life . . . Jesus. The affirmer. The embracer. The One who accepts us just as we are. The One who calls us out of darkness into His wonderful light (1 Peter 2:9).

HEALING PAIN FROM THE PAST

Jesus' healing power is often associated with light. The light of affirmation that we have just talked about is warm and inviting. I think of cold evenings when I used to hike the moors in England. At dusk the day grew dark; here and there the soft, diffuse lights of cozy cottages glowed like embers on the hillsides. Turning my collar up for warmth, I longed to be sitting by a fire at home in one of those cottages. Affirmation gives you that warm feeling of radiance and well-being.

That is one way God heals rejection. It is most often used to heal hurts on the surface, to meet an immediate need. Dave was bursting with pain; he needed to be held and comforted as a loving parent holds a sobbing child. His immediate need was met by being invited into the warmth of a caring community that offered him acceptance and unconditional love.

But often our hurts are not immediately evident on the surface of our minds and hearts. The tears have long dried, the crisis weathered, the pain forgotten . . . or is it? Psychologists tell us that everything that happens to us is stored in the memory bank of our subconscious, and whether we are aware of it or not, unhealed hurts from the past can still sabotage our present and future. How does God heal hidden pain from the past?

Again, the healing light is used, but in a different way. In recent years scientists have discovered and perfected a powerful beam of light, the laser, that can search the body very precisely, pinpoint a source of pain, and perform the necessary operation to heal diseased tissue. The Spirit of God is like that laser: it can search the deep recesses of the mind, locate a key memory, and let the presence of Jesus transform it with His love.

The healing of a memory is a specific kind of healing moment. It is often instrumental in healing rejection because rejection is often rooted in the past. I still remember vividly the first time Jesus came gently into my life and healed a forgotten hurt in this way. It happened long before I knew that God could really come personally to each of us and change those things in our lives that seem fixed forever, a permanent part of who we are.

The memory that God chose to heal on this occasion was twenty years old and it came to light in a most peculiar way. I was sitting in a living room with friends, sharing special times we felt close to our fathers. My friend, Lorna, outgoing and boisterous at seventy, told us that she loved playing basketball in high school and she still remembered the time her father sat in the stands watching her win a major tournament. She was so proud that her Dad was watching; she played a great game and was featured in the local paper the next day.

The memories that we shared that night were all warm and affectionate. As we drove away from the meeting, I should have been in good spirits. But I wasn't. I felt sick to my stomach and suddenly depressed. I didn't know why. As I thought about Lorna's story, I realized that it brought to mind the worst memories of my adolesence. I had played basketball too in school, but it was a humiliating and wounding experience.

During those awkward growing up years, I was tall and skinny, all arms and legs. At an age when developing bodies are the brunt of peer group jokes, I was constantly bombarded with jibes. Not only was I thin, but also flat-chested; I was terribly self-conscious about my appearance. To make matters worse, I hadn't gone to that school long and still felt ostracized as an outsider. My self-image was at an all time low.

These feelings of inferiority surfaced when I felt exposed in a public setting, which is what happened when I played on the basketball team. I liked playing basketball with neighborhood friends in our backyard, but when I found myself in a gym with a crowd watching, I felt paralyzed. I literally couldn't move. I would scoot to the end of the bench, hoping the coach would not send me into the game; if he did, I retreated to the farthest corner of the court, hoping no one would throw the ball to me; if they did, I just hugged the ball and hoped it would soon all be over!

I fell asleep that night, ruminating on these painful memories. Suddenly I found myself in the middle of a dream that focused all these memories into a single dramatic moment. I was playing basketball in the biggest game of the season. The gym was packed with spectators. The crowd in this particular gym sat above the court looking down on the game, which for me accentuated the pressure of the stares bearing down on me. I stood in the corner of the court, breaking out in a cold sweat, my knees shaking. I thought I was going to faint.

Someone threw me the ball. I froze. Then something extraordinary happened. I saw myself carrying the ball effortlessly toward the goal in a straight line right through the tangle of players. I felt lifted up, high over their heads. The next thing I saw was the basketball hoop beneath me. I dropped the ball easily through the basket to win the game. The crowd went wild! I felt ecstatic. I looked down, wondering why I found myself so high above the floor, and saw Jesus, smiling, carrying me on His shoulders. The dream ended there.

I woke up the next morning laughing to myself, incredibly happy, lighthearted as if some burden had been lifted from my mind. It had. Try as I might, I could not remember why those basketball memories had been so painful. I could only call to mind the joy of being lifted on Jesus' shoulders and how loved I felt at that moment. It was as if the old, wounding memories had been completely erased and replaced by a new set of mental pictures that were wonderfully affirming, rather than debilitating.

The core of my being was so profoundly touched by Jesus' affirmation and acceptance that not only was that one memory of rejection healed, but also that whole painful period of my life. In that moment, my self-image was fundamentally changed. I began to think of myself differently. As an adult I grew in confidence, no longer carrying around in my mind those inward feelings of inferiority that I had struggled with as an adolescent.

I noticed the biggest difference when I faced crowds as a teacher and public speaker. God had been wanting to grow these gifts in me; the key to their release was a healthy, relaxed self-image which began naturally to emerge once I was healed from that pain in my past. Instead of dreading people's attention, I learned to enjoy speaking in front of audiences. I am thoroughly convinced that one of the major factors for this change was that unusual memory healing.

"Inner healing is a process," writes Barbara Shlemon in her book *Healing the Hidden Self*. "No single prayer, spiritual exercise or meditative technique can possibly touch all the unhealed areas within us. The process of healing the inner person is a journey which we travel throughout our Christian lives as we gradually become infused with the light of God's love."[7]

Shlemon, of course, is right. No single healing moment, however significant, is sufficient to heal all of our hurts, but to experience just a little bit of that transforming power is to release more and more of that power in our lives.

We will discuss memory healing again in later chapters, but for now let's look at still another way that God heals rejection.

SEEING JESUS FACE TO FACE

So far we have talked about two ways God heals rejection: affirmation and memory healing. The examples I used were both serendipitous, unexpected; they suggest ways God takes the initiative to come to us. I encourage you to always be open to such occurrences. But I also want to describe a way that we can take the initiative by coming consciously into God's presence for healing.

To do this requires a special kind of prayer, which I call "interactive prayer," the process of picturing Jesus in Scripture by stepping into a biblical scene and, through the imagination, becoming an active participant in what you read, rather than a passive observer. In interactive prayer, Jesus invites us to see Him face to face, to feel His presence and to receive His love in our hearts as well as our minds.

We may be Christians all our lives, attending worship services, being diligent in prayer, studying the Bible. But as one writer observes, we may secretly confess: "I know God loves you, but knowing myself as I do, it is hard to believe he loves me."[8] We need to experience that love firsthand to truly believe it is ours.

Shelley first taught me this. I met Shelley at an inner healing retreat, a time of teaching and reflection that focuses on how personal hurt can be healed through prayer. During that weekend, I experienced Jesus' love and healing to a depth I'd never known before, and, in turn, I felt the conviction of the Holy Spirit calling me into the inner healing ministry myself.

Immediately, I found myself in Shelley's room. Shelley was a needy young woman who came late to the retreat. Someone gave her an armload of printed materials and she was lying on her bed trying to sort it all out when I knocked on her door. I asked if I could help explain what she was reading. We talked about her concept of God. She had none. If forced to be specific, she would characterize Him as harsh and judgmental, punishing.

When Shelley told me about her life, I could readily see why she viewed God this way. Even as a child, Shelley knew she was not wanted. Alcoholism and divorce haunted her background; her step-father was domineering and abusive. Shelley's heart had been beaten and battered like the peach we described earlier. As she poured out a lifetime of pain, I sighed inwardly. "Lord, how did I get into this? I don't know how to help Shelley." I wanted to walk out the door and never come back!

This was my human reaction. However, alongside my wavering sense of inadequacy, I felt a clear leading from the Holy Spirit. I didn't know what to do. He did. Gently, I helped Shelley see how God had cared for her despite so many bitter disappointments, providing her with a warm, church family and several close, supportive friends. Looking honestly at her relationship with God, Shelley admitted that she had been distant and withdrawn from Him, not letting Him love her.

Shelley needed to experience God's love in a tangible way. Like so many damaged men and women with wounded backgrounds, there was still inside Shelley a wounded little girl who had never known the love and acceptance of caring parents. This deep-rooted rejection was reinforced every time she experienced rejection again which led to internalized shame, "a sense of being uniquely and hopelessly flawed . . . different and less valuable than other human beings."[9] Shelley needed more than affirmation, more than the healing of one memory or even a set of memories to transform her wounded self-image. She needed a whole new picture of herself.

I sensed that God wanted to express His love to Shelley as a nurturing parent, to restore the experience of unconditional love that she missed as a child. Shelley did not need to be told how much God loved her; she needed to see that love with her own eyes and feel it with her whole being.

She was able to do this in interactive prayer. As Shelley and I closed our eyes in prayer, a familiar scene came to mind: the well-known incident in the Gospels where Jesus invites children to come to Him to sit in His lap. He holds them, lays loving hands on them, and blesses them. I asked Shelley if she could picture this scene; she had no trouble doing this. It is a warm story and easy to enter into.

We imagined Jesus sitting under a spreading oak on a summer day. Then we re-enacted the story, picturing Shelley as one of the children sitting at Jesus' feet. As the experience unfolded, Jesus decided to pick up a little curly-haired blonde girl, Shelley, out of all the children there. Shelley had been excluded all her life. Just to be singled out and chosen made her feel special.

Sitting in Jesus' lap as a child, Shelley imagined snuggling close to this friendly man, melting into the contours of His chest, feeling His hand stroke her cheek. She felt treasured, a sense of belonging.

I suggested that Shelley look up into Jesus' eyes. As she did this, she saw for the first time how precious and supremely valued she really was. There is tremendous power in seeing Jesus face to face. Our self-image is formed by the way other people see us. If other people, wounded themselves, project their own hurt onto us, or if we degrade ourselves, we are not seeing a true picture. These distorted pictures are a poor reflection of who we really are (1 Corinthians 13:12). To gaze clearly and directly into the face of the Lord of Love is to see ourselves as we really are, fully and deeply loved.

When we begin to realize that we are valued and esteemed, we begin to see ourselves differently. The masks fall away, the hardness, the hurt. This is what happened to Shelley. As she saw Jesus and the depth of His love for her, her countenance visibly changed. It softened, brightened. For a long, lingering moment Shelley just rested there, being filled up with Jesus' all-embracing love, tears quietly rolling down her cheeks.

This experience lasted only a short time, but when Shelley opened her eyes, her face was radiant. "Only as I receive God's love in my spirit," writes Margaret Therkelsen, "can I become the person he created me to be. Then can I know who I am in him . . . I feel valuable and worthwhile. My sense of self-esteem, built on his esteem for me, develops as his love reveals how precious I am."[10]

Was Shelley's healing moment just an emotional, short-lived experience or would it bring about lasting change? Only time would tell. Her transformation would be ongoing. As Scripture says, we are changed little by little into Christ's likeness as we behold His glory (2 Corinthians 3:18). Change is gradual, but it is sure. Destructive attitudes and habits need to be replaced by healthy ones; it takes time to learn new ways of relating and being. But knowing we are loved gives us the courage to change.

RECEIVING THE GIFT OF ACCEPTANCE

We are all valuable and worthwhile in God's eyes, but like Shelley, sometimes we need to *see* this and *feel* it to really believe it. Remember the question at the beginning of this chapter. "What is your greatest need?" Perhaps your deepest need is simply to know that you are loved just for who you are. You don't have to come from a dysfunctional background to need this reassurance. Even the most confident of us has a hunger to feel affirmed.

I've gone back many times in prayer to that familiar biblical story I shared with Shelley—imagining myself as a little child blessed by Jesus—to restore my own sense of wholeness and well-being. And I've shared that prayer since with many people like Shelley. Even though the scene is the same, it unfolds differently for each person who experiences it. Some people find it difficult to look into Jesus' eyes, but they can hear affection in His voice; others feel His love through touch.

I invite you now to receive the gift of acceptance by entering into your own personal prayer experience. Open up all your senses, your imagination. Come as a child, open, trusting, ready to receive God's love. "Draw near to God," says Scripture, "and He will draw near to you" (James 4:8). To prepare for the prayer time, these three steps, suggested by Richard Foster, are helpful:[11]

1. Center down—let go of outward distractions until you are completely still before God. Sit comfortably, relax, slowly letting all inner tension drain away.
2. Behold the Lord—draw close to God by focusing wholly on Him; picture Him as right there. Sense His nearness and love.
3. Listen—be inwardly attentive to what God wants to communicate. As you've tuned out external noises, be fully aware of gentle stirrings within. Foster describes this as "our spirit on tiptoe, alert and listening."

To Foster's list, I want to also suggest listening to worshipful music to provide a context for this kind of imaginative prayer. Sometimes silence is enough to draw us into a completely attentive, listening state; but music can also be a great help to relax our minds and spirits and release our imaginations.

You are now ready to enter into interactive prayer. On the next page, you'll find a scene described in Scripture, then a retelling of the narrative placing you in the center of the story.

Read the words first, then close your eyes. In silence or while listening to music, imagine yourself there. Let the action unfold in your mind. Slowly, gradually, let it draw you in . . .

THE GIFT
OF ACCEPTANCE

 Read and Reflect on Mark 10:13–16

Then they brought little children to Him, that He might touch them; but the disciples rebuked those who brought them. But when Jesus saw it, He was greatly displeased and said to them, "Let the little children come to Me, and do not forbid them; for of such is the kingdom of God. Assuredly, I say to you, whoever does not receive the kingdom of God as a little child will by no means enter it." And He took them up in His arms, laid His hands on them, and blessed them.

Picture yourself as a little child. You're tired, dirty from traveling dusty roads, trailing behind at the edge of the crowd. All day you've tried to keep up. Why are grown-ups always in a hurry?

Suddenly the jostling and constant movement of the crowd stops. As the mob presses in, there is anger, misunderstanding. You hear one man's voice above the crowd, firm, but gentle. He is a warm and friendly man. He sits down under a tree to rest; the crowd backs away. Timidly, curiously, the children come forward and sit in a circle at His feet.

One by one, He picks up each boy, each girl, even the babies, and holds them in His lap. What would it be like to have Him hold you? You glance down at the dirt, a little afraid, uncertain. He may not notice you at all. And what if He does? Will you go forward?

Just then, He looks your way and smiles. He stretches out His hand and invites you to come close. His hand is strong, tender, and you take it. You look up into His eyes. Soft, welcoming . . . The fear you felt earlier melts away.

He scoops you up into His arms. Relax. Lean back and rest your head on His broad shoulder. It feels so good just to rest. You didn't realize how tired you were. Tired . . . so tired. As you let go of your weariness, not just a physical weariness but a frazzled feeling inside, a kind of quiet strength seems to flow into you, a kind of peace.

Resting in Jesus' arms, you feel secure, protected. He tells you you are special, the apple of his eye. "_____ (insert your name), you are my beloved child. I love you. How precious you are. I love everything about you." He gently touches your nose, smiling at the freckles (which have always embarrassed you), stroking your hair (which you've always wished was blonde or brown or curly like someone else's). Jesus tells you that you are wonderful just the way you are. He tells you how much He loves you not only in words but in the way He holds you, the way He looks at you.

Time seems to stand still. You are all alone with Jesus now. The crowd has gone . . . somewhere. Their voices hushed. You wish you could rest here forever. Perhaps there are tears. That's okay. Let them come. You don't know why you're crying. It's just that you've never been loved this way and you wish it would last.

Jesus knows your longing. "Come back," He smiles. "Come back often. Whenever you choose to return, I will be here. I will always be here for you."

And you know, because you have grown to trust Him, that this is true. You can return in prayer anytime, whenever you are feeling broken or empty or unsure of yourself or just tired. He will always be here to rest and restore you in His embrace.

THE GIFT
OF NEW LIFE

"I am the resurrection and the life."

—*John 11:25*

*J*esus loves us just as we are, but He also longs to release and empower us to become everything we can be in Him. He came, He said, to give us an abundant life—life at its fullest, richest, most complete. The same "incomparably great power" that God used to raise Christ from the dead is available to all Christians, says Paul in Ephesians 1:19 (NIV), which means that the indwelling power of God is at work in us continually setting us free from anything that prevents us from being vibrant, responsive and fully alive.

"Therefore, if anyone is in Christ," Scripture declares, "he is a new creation; the old has gone, the new has come!" (2 Corinthians 5:17 NIV). Divine love inspires a life of ongoing, dynamic transformation and growth.

John and Paula Sanford in their book *The Transformation of the Inner Man,* point out that the word *salvation* does not simply mean "to be born again," but actually comes from a Hebrew root word meaning "to become whole, to be healed."[1] Being born anew then is not just a one-time event, "accepting Jesus into your life," but also day-by-day renewal and growth as we mature in Christ, receiving more of God's healing and becoming more whole persons. The good news is that the gift of new life that first thrills us upon conversion has within it even more gifts to discover.

The Bible calls this process of inner transformation "sanctification." I think of it as Jesus' love penetrating deeper and deeper into our hearts, liberating us to a greater and greater degree until we reflect God's glory more perfectly and discover who we were born to be. "Be transformed by the renewing of your mind," writes Paul. How do we do this? By presenting our bodies as "living sacrifices" (Romans 12:1–2). Dying to self paradoxically allows us to embrace more and more of what real living is.

OPENING UP

For me, parenting provides a perfect analogy for the transformation we are talking about. One Easter I was asked to give a talk to a parenting class at church. As I was driving around town doing my errands, the Holy Spirit gave me the title for the talk, "Parenthood and the Power of the Cross."

"You've got to be kidding!" I protested. "That doesn't sound very upbeat. I want something snappy and appealing. Positive." And yet as I began to think about it, I realized that parenting had been a deep process of change for me, painful at times, shattering, stretching as I let go of "self" and learned to love to a greater extent than I ever had before.

I did give the talk with that title. To illustrate the concept I used a nest of wooden eggs painted like bunnies. The egg is of course the symbol for Easter, representing the tomb opening up with a mysterious surprise within—death and resurrection. As I opened up the egg-shaped bunnies, each time revealing another nesting within, I reflected on how God had "opened me up" more and more to Himself, to myself, and to others during different stages of parenting.

The first smiling bunny looked smug, dressed slickly in a perfectly tied bow-tie. I thought of him as my hard outer shell, the ambitious, professional me, who had to give up my intact, independent lifestyle to become a mom. The next bunny was wide-eyed with a disheveled bow-tie: he was becoming more child-like, letting loose and beginning to enjoy parenthood just as I did. Then came a bunny who was learning the gift of compassion through tears; as he became more vulnerable, he heard the cries of others in pain. This new openness led me into ministry. The last little bunny, at the core of these personas, was the last to break, the "hardest nut to crack." It represented my innermost self, my own insecurities, my own neediness, that I came in touch with as I learned to parent. After opening up the most protected part of my heart to God's love, now empty, free, poured out, there was nothing left—or everything. As we completely let go of self, we become, as Macrina Wiederkehr says, "pure capacity for God."[2]

The message of the cross is that dying to self leads to new life. This is what parenthood taught me too. But this process of dying and being reborn only made sense as I looked back at the total experience. As I was going through those changes, I felt uncertain, desperate at times, fearful, angry. Rather than embracing the new, I clung to the old; rather than risking the unknown, I wanted to settle for what I was accustomed to. Change didn't come easily, but it did come through the grace of God.

And it will come for you. Like me, you may be fearful of change, yet there may also be within you a stirring, an inner impulse to embrace more of life than you do now. Trust that stirring. It is an invitation from One who calls you to reach beyond yourself, to enlarge your heart, to see with eyes of faith new possibilities within yourself and the world around you.

GETTING UNSTUCK

They say it is darkest just before dawn. What a glorious truth if you are living in the dawn, but what if you are still trapped in the dark? To use the Easter analogy, there are times when we feel "entombed." You know the feeling. We've all been there. Sometimes life can feel overwhelming; we feel trapped by problems, paralyzed by fear, isolated by depression. It is a dark and lonely place to be.

This feeling of "stuckness" may last for days, or months, even years. We can get stuck at any stage in our faith journeys. "Getting stuck occurs sometimes from our fear of facing the unknown," say Janet Hagberg and Bob Guelich.[3] "Other times it results from personal or work crises that we cannot control. Sometimes an illness or death causes us to feel abandoned, thus making us vulnerable to being stuck. Even memories of negative events or relationships, perhaps from our childhood, can surface, and in our fear of facing them, we become stuck. It may even be that we are simply afraid to face the fact that we are loved unconditionally by God. Accepting that means admitting we cannot control God or our destiny."

Do you feel trapped by circumstances? Hemmed in? Immobilized? In the midst of our despair, the Lord of Life declares, "Behold, I make all things new!" (Revelation 21:5). Is that what you long for? A new beginning. In this chapter we'll explore what hinders us from living life to the fullest as Jesus intended and how healing can help us move beyond the "stuck" places in our lives.

CHANGE ME, LORD

Ginny longed for a new beginning. She longed for it desperately. Ginny was a staff worker in a mission organization: her life was supposed to reflect the love and joy of Jesus. Outwardly it did, but inwardly she was falling apart. Ginny had grown up in a family with the "no-talk" rule. If you had problems, you "stuffed them." So that was what she did. No one knew about her inner turmoil.

Ginny was stuck. "I felt like I was in a whirlpool . . . going around and around with no way to get out. Joyless, prayerless, unfruitful, empty, dry, parched, struggling would pretty well describe the 'real' me that I had to try to keep hidden," Ginny remembers. "I'd kept the 'correct mask' on for so long, that no one knew who I really was and there seemed to be no way of getting beyond that place. I even began to wonder who I really was."

Ginny lived a life of utter weariness—going through the motions and being careful to keep her mask in place, trying to convince herself and everyone else that all was well . Gradually Ginny slipped into depression. She couldn't eat or sleep. She was fortunate to get three or four hours sleep at night and those hours were constantly interrupted. Constant aching and pain drained her of energy and enthusiasm. "My Christian life reached the point of bankruptcy in every area—physically, mentally, emotionally and spiritually." During those dark days, Ginny would be driving down the street and suddenly break down sobbing. "Change me, Lord," she pleaded, "please change me."

On a summer night in 1990 that prayer was answered. Ginny had gone with a group of friends to a prayer conference. It was a large conference, filling an auditorium with thousands of people.

After a teaching session, an invitation was given for people to come forward for prayer for personal needs. One by one, they did get up from their seats and make their way up to the front of the room. Ginny had a sense that she should ask for prayer. But she ignored that sense. Then she heard an inner voice: "Ginny, you can sit here and leave the same person you are now, or you can go forward for prayer."

Ginny still stayed glued to her seat, embarrassed to let her friends know that she had a problem. After all, she had been a Christian for forty years and a Christian staff worker for twenty. What would they think? One sensitive friend discerned that Ginny had a need and put her hand on hers gently. "I think you should go forward for prayer, Gin."

Ginny still didn't move. If she had a problem, what was it? What did she need prayer for? She had plenty of problems—insomnia, overeating, depression—but God seemed to be revealing that there was a root problem. Ginny asked frantically, "What is it, Lord?"

"And just like that I knew," she said, "so plainly and clearly . . . I knew God loved me, but that head knowledge wouldn't come down into my heart. I didn't love myself and that made it impossible for me to believe that He or anyone else could love me either. It also made it impossible for me to express my love to anyone. I couldn't tell God I loved Him; I couldn't even tell my mother I loved her."

By this time, some of Ginny's friends came close and helped her move toward the front of the room. One of them went and got the man who had spoken that night and asked him to pray for Ginny. The prayer lasted about twenty minutes and she couldn't remember what the man prayed exactly, but as he prayed, she felt a deep, deep cleansing, a washing out of hurt and anguish she had repressed for years. Ginny sobbed uncontrollably. Now what would her friends think! On the way to the conference, Ginny had said, "Why do people have to be so emotional when they pray? I'm not comfortable with so much emotion."

Ginny smiled, remembering that incredible night. "I was crying at top volume. Part of me said, 'Ginny, you're making a fool of yourself.' The other part said, 'I don't care!'"

As she was being prayed for, Ginny heard Jesus tenderly speaking to her, "I love you, Ginny. I love you." She wanted to respond and express her love to Him. It was a struggle, a battle, that literally brought her to her knees. Finally she was able to say the words out loud. "Oh, I love you, Lord! I love you!" She heard herself saying those words over and over again to Him.

At that moment Ginny saw Jesus in her mind's eye, just the hem of His garment and His sandals.

"He was so close. I felt myself reaching out and touching Jesus like the woman with the hemorrhage who had reached out in a crowd to touch Him and been healed."

As she saw this, she leaned forward, literally reaching out. Then she drew back. A friend, recognizing her hesitancy, said: "Don't stop short, Ginny. Don't stop short of everything God has for you."

Ginny reached out again. "The second time I felt I really touched Him," she remembers. "He wasn't beyond me anymore." As soon as Ginny felt this, the power of that moment in prayer that had come on so suddenly with such force ebbed away. "It was as if power really did flow out of Him and into me just as the story says."

Ginny felt a total release from the burden of secret pain she had carried so long. "I felt such freedom, as if heavy chains had fallen off. 'I'll never be the same again!' I told my friends." Bubbles of joy welled up inside of Ginny; she began to laugh and laugh and couldn't stop. "I could have flown," said Ginny, remembering her feeling of exhilaration.

A NEW NAME

When Ginny returned to the mission organization where she worked, she felt she should "keep the lid on" about what happened. No one would understand and she didn't want to "act like a lunatic." But she couldn't help smiling and showing her joy. She had good reason to rejoice. She felt like a new person! Her insomnia ended and depression lifted. With long peaceful nights of sleep and her constant negative thinking ended, she felt energized. As well as being renewed physically and emotionally, spiritually she enjoyed her own "personal revival." The Bible, which used to appear simply as black letters on a white page, suddenly came alive. "I was filled with the joy of the Lord."

Finally, at a Thanksgiving service she decided to share publicly what had happened. She confessed how difficult it had been to admit her neediness; but once she let go of her pride, God was able to heal her woundedness. "God has radically changed my life," she said. "I'm not the same person I was a few months ago or the same person I was yesterday. He has given me a new name."

Ginny read the words of a song that described the way she felt:

> I will change your name
> You will no longer be called
> wounded, outcast, lonely or afraid.
>
> I will change your name
> Your new name will be
> Confidence, Joyfulness, Overcoming One,
> Faithfulness, Friend of God, One Who seeks my
> face![4]

Ginny's public testimony sent a shock wave through that place of "good people." The phone began to ring. Friends began to approach her privately, sharing their hidden pain. Again and again, she heard: "Ginny, I want the freedom and joy you have. That's what I'm hungry for too."

As radical as the changes were in Ginny's life, there were more to come. God revealed to Ginny that what had been healed was only the "tip of the iceberg." It is often the case that God reveals His love for us in a powerful way so that we have the strength to face and resolve issues in our lives that continue to cause hidden pain and hinder our growth. In Ginny's case, God slowly, tenderly began to reveal that her low self-esteem and inability to risk intimacy in relationships which had caused her depression was due to buried childhood physical and sexual abuse.

Ginny had denied, run from, and smoothed over those hurtful memories all her life in an effort to survive. Through the help of a Christian support group, Ginny learned to face the pain, forgive those who had hurt her, and correct the unhealthy patterns of coping behavior that were creating relational problems for her as an adult. One ray of truth that really stuck with her from that group was the statement: "Your burdens are only as heavy as the secrets you keep."

With the help of God's love and a group of caring people who listened, affirmed, and loved unconditionally, Ginny was able to let the truth unlock the secrets of the past. "Denial had held me captive," said Ginny. "Things in my mind got darker and deeper because I wouldn't let any light shine in. When I learned to face the issues, I discovered they weren't so bad and they were workable. And one at a time I worked through them." A year after she had come frightened and hesitant to the group, Ginny became a group leader, helping others find healing.

Today Ginny is still changing. One of the greatest changes she finds is a new desire to know God more deeply, to read the Word and become acquainted with this heavenly Father who loves her so completely. "Everything I read tells me again and again of His love and acceptance, of His awareness of everything that has made me me. He knows of the hurts that caused the scars, the flaws and imperfections and He loves me anyway.

"He has given me hope, love, passion for living life to the fullest, and a desire to share with others the fact that there is hope for new life—no matter how long we may have been walking around without it."

Every morning when Ginny starts work, she glances at a picture above her desk and smiles. The vibrant print of "Jesus Laughing" shows Jesus throwing his head back, his mouth opened wide in exuberant laughter. It reminds Ginny of the total freedom and joy she felt that September night in 1990 when she experienced an incredible moment of transformation that gave her a new beginning and launched her on a journey of greater and greater growth.

ROADBLOCKS TO CHANGE AND GROWTH

Let's look at Ginny's story in light of the two questions we asked at the beginning of this chapter. First, what prevents us from living life to the fullest as Jesus intended? And secondly, how can healing help us move beyond the stuck places in our lives?

It might appear as if Ginny's healing moment "just happened." She was in the right place at the right time. She was lucky. But Ginny doesn't see it that way. "Looking back over the years, I now realize that God never quit drawing my heart toward Him. So many entries in my journals show His drawing me and my longing toward Him. There were times of starting toward Him, only to give up and fall back into self-effort, self-protection. I just never knew how to go forward."

It seems clear from Ginny's reflection that God had been trying to draw Ginny close for a long time. But she was unable to respond. Why? As Jesus stood outside Lazarus' tomb and called him from death to life, He comes seeking us in our dark and lonely places, our stuck places, and calls us by name: "Ginny, come out!" What prevents us from taking a step toward him? Let's explore some reasons:

1. **Fear.** We are afraid of change. Studies show that in unhealthy situations—dysfunctional homes of alcohol, abuse, even violence—people often choose to stay in those situations, no matter how painful they are, because that is all

they've known. It is hard to imagine anything else, and it is hard to face the discomfort of changing. This was Ginny's "self-protection."

2. **Pride**. Ginny was embarrassed to admit to herself, a good Christian, and to her friends, who appeared to have no problems of their own, that she was miserable. "I didn't want to think of myself as bad," Ginny said, "and tell my garbage to other people." Ironically, when she did share her brokenness publicly, many around her began to share their hidden pain too.

3. **Self-Effort**. Ginny, as good Christians often do, tried to read the Bible more, pray more, do all the right things, to feel better about herself. She became exhausted trying in her own strength to solve her problems. When at last help came, she thought of it as a "miracle of grace."

4. **Unworthiness**. Even though Ginny longed for a more intimate relationship with God, in her heart of hearts she didn't believe she was worthy of God's love. "I didn't blame Him for not loving me," said Ginny. "Why would He?"

5. **Confusion**. Ginny remained stuck, immobilized by her pain. "I just never knew how to go forward," she remembers. When we sink into the darkness of self-condemnation, we loose our sense of direction and can't take a step in *any* direction.

Can you identify with any of these roadblocks to change and growth? I can. At different times in my life (even at different times during the day!) I find myself throwing up these blockades. They are the human defenses we all hide behind. These coping mechanisms—that protect us from hurt, keep us intact, keep us in control—are so ingrained and thoroughly a part of us that we resort to them without even thinking. They may be necessary when we are in danger, but they can also prevent us from becoming vulnerable when it is safe to trust.

And yet there are moments, graced moments, when all our defenses are swept aside and God's love flows into our lives unimpeded. The walls come tumbling down and light floods in. The Spirit of the living God falls afresh on us, melting, molding, reshaping, fashioning something new. This is the gift of new life.

SAYING YES TO CHANGE

"God draws us to Himself," says Ginny, "but we have to say yes." Yes and yes and yes at every turn because the inner transformation that God calls us to is an ongoing process and is always much bigger than we imagine. How did God's healing help Ginny keep saying yes to change and growth even though she was fearful and resisted it at first? Let's look at the five roadblocks and how they were each overcome:

1. **Fear.** "Perfect love casts out fear," says Scripture (1 John 4:18). God's healing came first as a deep and overwhelming sense of how much He loved Ginny. That love filled her so completely that it literally pushed out the fear that kept her immobilized. She experienced it as a deep cleansing and infilling of love and joy. It released her to say yes to change.
2. **Pride.** Once Ginny had experienced God's unconditional love, she was free to accept herself completely—shadow side and all. She became more real and transparent and didn't feel a need to hide behind a facade. No longer fixed by a narrow self-concept, she became more open to new possibilites in herself and others.
3. **Self-Effort.** Ginny thought of her healing moment as a

"love gift." It came unexpectedly. She didn't earn it. She would never really understand it, but she didn't have to. It was hers to accept freely. She began to rest in her faith, not work at it, and be more open to these moments as simply an outpouring of God's love.

4. **Unworthiness.** Ginny began to find her worth in God's love, not in her own goodness. When she was tempted to wound herself with self-condemnation, she only had to raise her gaze to see the way the Father looked at her in Christ. "There is therefore now no condemnation to those who are in Christ Jesus" (Romans 8:1).

5. **Confusion.** As Ginny saw herself more clearly in Jesus, He showed her the way to greater maturity in Him. She had the courage to ask for help, and she found it in the form of specific resources: books, tapes and a support group who encouraged her on her road to growth.

One of the greatest resources God provides to help us grow and change is the gift of other Christians. "The folks in my support group," said Ginny, "seemed to understand what I was trying to express. They listened, affirmed and loved me unconditionally. No rejection. No judgment. They understood." We need each other. Risking change, becoming something new, is scary business. As we risk vulnerability and open ourselves to the new life God calls us to, we need warm words of encouragement every step along the way; we need hugs and embraces and an ongoing commitment from friends who will see us through.

ARE YOU FIXED FOREVER?

It is a lie to think we cannot change. Certainly we can choose to believe negative, self-deprecating self-talk: "I'll never change. That's just the way I am." Or we can choose to let other people fix us with judgment or let circumstances limit who we are. As this modern poet suggests, we may feel sometimes as if we are mercilessly paralyzed by the past:

> God snaps your picture—don't look away—
> this room right now, your face tilted
> exactly as it is before you can think
> or control it. Go ahead, let it betray
> all the secret emergencies and still hold
> that partial disguise you call your character.

> Even your lip, they say, the way it curves
> or doesn't, or can't decide, will deliver
> bales of evidence. The camera, wide open,
> stands ready; the exposure is thirty-five years
> or so—after that you have become
> whatever the veneer is, all the way through.

> Now you want to explain. Your mother
> was a certain—how to express it—*influence*.
> Yes. And your father, whatever he was,
> you couldn't change that. No. And your town
> of course had its limits. Go on, keep talking—
> Hold it. Don't move. That's you forever.[5]

Are we fixed forever? Not at all, according to the Bible. "Now the Lord is the Spirit, and where the Spirit is, there is freedom. And we, who with unveiled faces all reflect the Lord's glory, are being transformed into his likeness with ever-increasing glory . . . inwardly we are being renewed day by day" (2 Corinthians 3:17–18; 4:16 NIV).

Does this sound like a God who snaps your picture, capturing a single, fixed image of who you are, and calls it quits? Quite the contrary! God's timetable is very different from our own. In our temporal view, the length of exposure to capture our likeness may seem like "thirty-five years or so," as the poet says, but God's timetable is eternity. The likeness He is bringing out in us is not just our character, but also His own.

"Beloved," writes John, "now we are children of God, and *it has not yet been revealed what we shall be,* but we know that when He is revealed, we shall be like Him, for we shall see Him as He is" (1 John 3:2, italics added). This verse suggests to me that transformation for Christians is an ongoing process that continues throughout our lives and is never complete until we see Christ face to face in heaven and fully reflect His glory.

What an incredible truth! This means that we are never fixed forever in our stuck places. "We are *being* transformed . . . inwardly renewed day by day." Even though this is true, we have to believe it and act on it, which is often a struggle. We have to choose to keep our minds focused on Christ instead of on circumstances, other people's opinions, and our own self-defeating attitudes. This is so difficult at times, it may feel as if a battle is being waged within us. It is.

AN AGE-OLD BATTLE

We mentioned at the outset of this chapter that Jesus comes into our lives to empower us to live fuller lives. At the same time, Jesus tells us, Satan comes like a thief in the night to steal and kill and destroy, to trap us in the darkness of our minds and paralyze our spirits. To immobilize us.

"Hell," wrote Charles Williams, "is an image that bears no more becoming."[6]

As Jesus inspires us to greater growth, Satan does the opposite: he appeals to our natural fears and insecurities to blind us to the possibility of change. Whereas Jesus, filling us with his love and helping us to see life as good, encourages us to take risks; Satan, filling us with self-defeating thoughts and feelings, helps get us stuck in the mire of despair. This means that everything we think or feel has a spiritual dimension to it.

We live out our lives in the context of a spiritual battle whether we recognize it or not. The battle between life and death, light and darkness. It is an age-old battle, a battle that is already won. However, even though Christ conquered the forces of death at the cross, we still have to appropriate that truth daily as we live out our lives now.

"I have set before you life and death," God said to the Israelites, "blessing and cursing; therefore choose life . . ." (Deuteronomy 30:19). His words are also addressed to us. Every day we have a choice: to move out in faith, or stay stuck in a "comfortable" situation that may be destructive to ourselves and others; to choose a new way or settle for the old ways of thinking and doing things even if they enslave us; to say yes to change even though this may mean facing our deepest fears and insecurities.

CHOOSE LIFE!

What about you? Is God calling you to new life, to step out in faith in a new way? You may feel stuck as Ginny did, just going through the motions of life, hiding behind a facade, lacking joy and power. Or perhaps you've just never felt fully alive. "It's as if part of me is dead," said a friend of mine, trying to explain the vague ache of only half-living. "It's as if I've never really lived out of the fullness of who I am."

"I am the resurrection and the life," says Jesus (John 11:25). Let the Lord of Life call you to new life in Him.

THE GIFT
OF NEW LIFE

 ead and Reflect
on John 11:1–44 (NIV)

Jesus, once more deeply moved, came to the tomb. It was a cave with a stone laid across the entrance. "Take away the stone," he said. . . . When he had said this, Jesus called in a loud voice, "Lazarus, come out!" The dead man came out, his hands and feet wrapped with strips of linen, and a cloth around his face. Jesus said to them "Take off the grave clothes and let him go" (vv. 38–39, 43–44).

Picture yourself as Lazarus, trapped in a dark tomb. You feel alone, forgotten, cast aside. There was the sickness, the long sickness, and then . . . the sound of the big stone being rolled in place, sealing off the light. Your heart sinks. It was so final, so irrevocable. You feel so cut off from the world, other people, yourself. Outside life goes on: everyone goes about their business. No one seems to notice that you're imprisoned here, no one seems to care.

You're swallowed up in the darkness, believing depression's lies. The darkness is heavy, oppressive, darker than night. You cannot see your hand in front of your face. It is that dark. A sea of darkness with no reference point, and no way out.

You have no idea how long you've been here. It seems interminable. In the darkness, a turmoil of angry thoughts stirs up resentment, bitterness. You feel betrayed. "If you love me, Lord, why did you let this happen? Where were you when I needed you? Where are you . . . are you . . . are you?" Taunting echoes bounce back at you from the dark cave walls.

However, even as you cry out, help is on its way. Just as Lazarus was not aware of the forces being marshalled on his behalf—the servants who ran to get Jesus, Mary and Martha who compelled Him to come—there are often people in our lives who are pleading for God to bring healing. Do you have friends, family, acquaintances who have shown they really do care? Perhaps they've prayed for you or with you; perhaps they've offered hugs or words of encouragement or listened with love when you've felt despondent.

Take a moment to imagine who these friends might be . . . Say their names, picture their faces. Soak up the love you see there. Have you ever told them you love them and expressed your gratitude?

Outside the tomb, the One who loves you the most is moved to tears. How grieved Love is when hurt condemns us to our dark and lonely places. It is our need that draws Him there, His compassion.

Into your darkness, He speaks a word of hope: "I am the resurrection and the life. He who believes in Me will live, even though he dies." Jesus looks heavenward, seeking the help of the Father. He orders the stone rolled away. Are there stones in your life that need to be removed? What are they? How might Jesus remove them?

Listen to Love Himself speak your name. "_____ (insert your name), come out!"

Jesus is the light of the world. As the stone is removed, His light floods in the tomb and dispells the darkness. You feel a stirring, an awakening of your spirit. You take a step forward. First one, then two. A new force is gathering in your heart: "I want to live! I want to live!"

As you walk out of the cave, your lungs are suddenly filled with fresh air. It is an exhilarating feeling, as if you can breathe again. You feel a resurrection-like surge of pleasure: the air is fragrant with the scent of spring, the earth, newly washed with rain . . . the freedom even to walk about fills you with gratitude.

The warmth of sunlight penetrates your bandages. What you feel is more than a physical sensation; it is also the warmth of human company. Dimly, through the cloth over your face, you can see people standing around you. Friends, loved ones. You can sense their closeness. Tenderly, they remove the grave clothes.

But it is Jesus who removes the linen from your face. Once free, you stand in front of Him face-to-face. Look into Jesus' eyes. What do you see? How do you feel?

It is more than freedom that He calls you to. It is deep communion with Him. A love relationship. See the desire in His eyes for you, His joy. His desire creates a longing in you to know and enjoy Him. There is laughter in His eyes and delight.

"Come, my friend," He seems to say. "We have a lot of living to do!"

THE GIFT
OF HEALING

*"I have heard your prayer, I have seen your tears;
surely I will heal you."*

—*2 Kings 20:5*

I can still see my three-year-old bursting out the door after a
long, cold Minnesota winter, running as fast as she can
down our asphalt driveway in a new pair of shorts. It's spring!
She flings out her arms, a big grin on her face, embracing all
the world in her bravado. Then, as suddenly as she leaves the
earth on wings, she comes crashing to the ground. As I scoop
her up and rock her in my arms, her crying quiets to a whimper.

This scene happened year after year during my daughter's
preschool years. I always tried to stop her from darting out of
the door, but she was too quick and defiant. So for a while our
springtimes began with tears and the piercing pain of scraped
knees.

We are human and we hurt. There are tears from physical

pain as our bodies bruise; silent sobs from heartbreak; deep distress from wrenching spiritual pain we aren't even aware of. God hears our prayers, sees our tears, and as I scooped up my little girl to offer comfort, so the heavenly Father responds in love to heal our hurts.

The picture of a mother calming a crying child in her arms is for me the simplest, most tangible picture of the way God heals. That may not be a picture that communicates to you, but it works for me because I'm a mom. Although we tend to think of healing as mystical, I believe our loving heavenly Father longs to show us what it is in concrete ways we all can understand.

Certainly, as a friend, you may have felt an impulse to reach out and touch a neighbor who comes to share a cup of coffee but begins to share a heart hurt that suddenly surfaces. Or you may have sensed rejection in a workmate's eyes as a wounding word is taken in; instinctively you know that encouragement is needed to salve that wound. Or it may be that in your busy life you somehow sense it is time to make a space, to offer a set-aside time sacrificially, to listen to the struggles of your teenager.

This is what human compassion looks like. God's love is not that different: it doesn't feel that different, it isn't offered that differently. God uses our natural channel of love and caring as a conduit for His divine intentions. However, when the supernatural quality of His love flows through these actions or these words, healing can penetrate deeper and do much more far-reaching work than we can imagine.

God hears our prayers and sees our tears and longs to touch our pain. He aches to hold us when we hurt and to let us know how deeply we are loved. He wants to show us His love personally, so He sends people into our lives to embody His love, to give a hug, to take a hand, come close and listen. Christianity is incarnational. "The Spirit longs to be enfleshed," writes Walter Wink.[1] God so longs to impress this truth upon our hearts that He sent Jesus to reveal, as clearly as He could, what His love looked like. "For God so loved the world that He gave His only begotten Son . . ." (John 3:16). Indeed, Jesus was called *Immanuel*—God with us. Jesus demonstrated a love the world had never seen, a love that is still operative in the world today.

If we want to discover how God heals, the best place to start is to open the living pages of Scripture and see how God expressed his love to hurting men and women through Jesus. I realize that some Christians believe that the way Jesus healed people in the Bible can't possibly happen now. In our modern culture, we don't see lepers walking around in rags, the crippled carried on stretchers, demoniacs living in caves. Surely those stories were written in a different context for a different time.

Were they? Are our needs that different than they were then? A person struggling with cancer or AIDS or Parkinson's knows what it feels like to feel untouchable: to lose all physical attractiveness and self-worth, to be rejected by friends and family. There are those who feel emotionally crippled from damaging childhood experiences, abuse or divorce. And there are some men and women who are so wounded from life's injustices that inner rage sometimes threatens to tear them apart.

I believe that Jesus comes today, just as He did to people two thousand years ago, to a world of dark and desperate need. Scripture says that Jesus is the same yesterday, today, and tomorrow (Hebrews 13:8). Let's look at Jesus' healing ministry for a moment. It will give us clues to understand how God heals today. Jesus' ministry on earth was very brief: just three years, a little more than a thousand days. But what a dramatic three years they were.

HOW DID JESUS HEAL?

Jesus was a man who loved people and loved life. He described Himself as the light of the world. The vibrance. The radiance. The giver of abundant life. "I have come that they may have life, and that they may have it more abundantly," He declared boldly (John 10:10). He came to liberate men and women from all that oppressed them.

This desire drove Him straight into the heart of darkness, the core of human suffering where His love was most needed. He knew there was another force at work in the world, and He came to defeat it. Jesus was the long-awaited Messiah, the Savior, who came to "heal the brokenhearted, to proclaim liberty to the captives and recovery of sight to the blind, to set at liberty those who are oppressed" (Luke 4:18–19).

These were more than mere words. Jesus backed up His claims by a forceful ministry that demonstrated His compassion and authority over the powers of darkness that ravaged human happiness. Wherever He went, He set people free from pain and disease. He touched a blind man who then could see; He touched the deaf and they could hear; He touched the dumb and they could speak. He touched the tormented and demons fled. He reached out His hand in forgiveness, which to some was the greatest gift of all.

When people witnessed these "signs and wonders," Jesus said, they would know that the kingdom of God was close at hand. God's will would be done on earth as it was in heaven. Indeed, where Jesus walked, the kingdom of God *was* at hand because He *was* the kingdom of God. God is love and Jesus was love personified.

These miraculous signs were visible evidence of the supernatural power Jesus spoke of in his teachings: "With God all things are possible" (Matthew 19:26). They were not performed like circus acts to entertain but were rather expressions of a loving God who longed to meet human need very specifically and very personally. People were moved by these miracles; moved to believe that God was perhaps not distant or made of stone but could actually be actively involved in their lives.

Jesus healed people in a variety of ways. His most common method of healing was the "laying on of hands." "All those who had any that were sick with various diseases brought them to Him; and He laid His hands on every one of them and healed them" (Luke 4:40). When Jesus instructed His disciples to carry on His healing ministry after He was gone, He told them to lay hands on the sick and these miracles would continue.

It was God's love that healed, not physical touch itself, but there was something about the warm touch of an ordinary human hand that communicated caring to the sufferer. Certainly this must have been reassuring and nurtured trust. Also, physical touch seemed to provide an interface, "a point of contact," between the spiritual and earthly, the divine and human, and helped put Jesus "in touch" with the unique needs of each individual.

Each of Jesus' healings was an "original masterpiece," says Michael Harper. "He treated each person differently, thus recognizing the individuality of each person and respecting it."[2] Harper also points out that this attentiveness to individual cases also demonstrated Jesus' total dependence on the Holy Spirit.

Jesus knew what was in the heart of each human being (John 2:25). In some cases He healed with straightforward laying on of hands. In other cases, He asked the sufferer penetrating questions. "Do you really want to get well?" He asked a man who had been lame for thirty-eight years and perhaps had become addicted to his illness. In other instances, He asked sufferers to be active participants in their healing to increase their faith: a woman with a withered hand was asked to stretch out her hand toward Jesus to receive His touch; a blind man was told to go and wash his eyes in a pool of water after Jesus had put mud on the man's eyes.

Often Jesus' healings were multifaceted: not only releasing someone from a physical handicap but also discerning and liberating a sin-sick heart or victim of demonic powers. The most celebrated healing miracle tells the story of a crippled man who was let down through a roof on a mat by four faithful friends. The man was healed of his crippledness: he rolled up his mat and went home rejoicing. This was spectacular and dramatic. But an overlooked part of the story is that Jesus forgave the man's sins first. Healing the heart, Jesus intimated, is often more difficult than healing the body.

Sometimes Jesus discerned spiritual forces at work in disease and oppression. In one instance, Jesus' disciples failed to heal a boy with epilepsy perhaps because they did not diagnose the root cause of the problem: an evil spirit. As soon as Jesus rebuked the demon, the boy was cured instantly. Deliverance from evil spirits, or exorcism, which may seem a bit bizarre to modern readers, was simply one of several tools that Jesus used to heal when it was necessary.

Most of the people Jesus reached out to heal were considered outcasts. Untouchables. The sick rejected by a healthy society, prostitutes and sinners kept at a distance by the righteous, the mentally ill whose mad behavior banished them from human company. Jesus felt particular compassion for those whom others regarded as hopeless—"the throwaways of society," as Mother Teresa calls them today.

Jesus seemed to be making the point by His actions as well as by His words that the kingdom of God was for everyone, especially those who felt unwanted and unloved. His touch affirmed all men and women as made in the image of God and therefore of infinite worth.

This is the "good news" of the gospel. This good news was for everyone, not just a chosen few. So from the very beginning of Jesus' ministry, He invited friends to draw close to him, "disciples," learners whom He began training to carry on His work.

First there were twelve. Jesus gave his disciples the authority to heal and cast out demons just as He did. As the work grew, Jesus appointed seventy-two others to go from town to town sharing His ministry: "Heal the sick who are there and tell them, 'The kingdom of God is near you'" (Luke10:9 NIV). They returned rejoicing, amazed that what Jesus said was true.

At the end of Jesus' ministry, He commissioned His disciples to go into all the world and preach the gospel. He promised that as they did this, miraculous signs would accompany their preaching, including healing the sick (Mark 16:18). Jesus promised to be with them "even to the end of the age" through the gift of the Holy Spirit. Finally, at Pentecost, the Holy Spirit was poured out not only on them, but on *all* believers, men and women, young and old—for all generations to come (Acts 2:17). The Holy Spirit which empowered Jesus and those early believers is a gift meant also for us.

HOW DOES GOD HEAL TODAY?

To think that God's healing could be as available to us as it was when Jesus walked the earth boggles the mind. "It's awesome," as my kids would say. And yet why shouldn't we believe it? God's purpose in healing the sick is the same today as it was in the Bible: to bring His kingdom near to us.

I first began to discover this years ago as I met with a group of friends who wanted to live their faith more intentionally. One member of the group wanted to study what the Bible had to say about healing. We started by studying verses pertaining to it. "Pray for one another, that you may be healed," says James 5:16. The Bible was very clear that Christians should pray for one another and their prayers would be answered.

I had never looked very closely at what the Bible said about healing. I had grown up in conservative evangelical churches that taught that the healing miracles were performed by Jesus and His disciples to demonstrate God's power in that day and age. I never seriously considered that that power was meant to be used today.

Other members of our group were from different traditions. They came from churches that included "healing services" as part of their Sunday morning worship. As children, they had seen people healed, but they didn't fully understand it. We were all wondering how this could be applicable to our own lives.

So we began to explore the subject together. We invited a young man to our group who had been healed through prayer when another Christian had "laid hands on him" as Jesus as had done in the Bible. John described a warmth flowing from his friend's hand into his aching back as his friend had prayed. Immediately the pain ceased.

This was remarkable to me. It meant that spiritual healing could be tangible and actually felt—a supernatural power that could be observed in the natural world. It was real.

John smiled when I said this. His parents had been missionaries in a remote village in Ecuador, South America for twenty-five years. He had learned that in third-world cultures, the spiritual side of life is very real. Doing ministry there, his parents immediately encountered dark spiritual forces pitted against them, even as Jesus did. But the exciting thing was once the villagers became Christians, they put the Bible into practice, believing exactly what it said, and like the early church in Acts, they experienced spiritual healings and other miracles.

As we continued our study of healing, we invited a woman to the group who was experienced in healing prayer. She explained that healing was just one of many spiritual gifts given to Christians—lay people as well as pastors—as they reached out to express God's love to people in need. She told us that some Christians actually develop a ministry of healing, but all Christians could be given the gift for particular situations of need. She encouraged us to begin by praying for each other.

Then she demonstrated how we could do this. Putting a chair in the center of the living room where we were meeting, she invited a volunteer to sit down and receive a prayer for healing. Then she invited the rest of us to gather around and put our hands on the person being prayed for. We each prayed aloud following her lead.

At first, we were timid and hesitant as we prayed. "If it be thy will, Lord, please help Jean to get well." Helen was stern with us, encouraging us to pray with greater confidence. Of course God wanted Jean to get well! How that might happen and when we didn't know, but we should assume that God's normal desire was for health and healing. I had never thought about this before, but it made sense to me. As a loving parent, I wanted my children to get well when they were sick; how much more must our loving heavenly Father desire the best for us.

The essence of healing prayer, said Helen, was entering into God's will, seeing the person well as God wanted her to be, and praying with Jesus' authority that God's will would come about.

Instead of concentrating on the problem, the sickness, we began to focus on God's healing. For example, we imagined the love of God flowing into the person's body and soothing a sore throat, destroying the germs that caused the infection, and restoring full health to the affected tissues.

PUT TO THE TEST

For several weeks at the end of our group meetings we prayed for one another as Helen had taught us. One couple reported that they had prayed for their two-year-old who had a high fever during the night. The next day the fever went down. We experienced small successes like this, but the real test came as we felt led to pray for an elderly man in our church who had had a cerebral hemorrhage. Venturing beyond this small circle of close friends to pray for a stranger in a hospital terrified me. What if nothing happened? What if he thought we were crazy?

On Easter night, my friends and I headed for the hospital. Harold was delighted that we had come. We talked a while, then someone found the courage to ask Harold if we could lay hands on him and pray for healing. "Sure," he grinned. "Just like Jesus did." So we gathered around and prayed for this wonderful, humble man, letting the Holy Spirit's warmth gently flow through our hands and praying in our own words. Harold was in such high spirits when we left, I thought he was instantly healed. My feeling of dread was replaced with euphoria. It was so exciting to be part of a miracle!

However, as I was to learn through many experiences of healing prayer, "hit-and-run" prayers are rarely the norm. The next day the news about Harold couldn't have been worse. He was paralyzed; he couldn't even speak or lift his head. I was stunned. My feeling of euphoria suddenly turned to depression. I felt betrayed. Why did God let us down?

Despite my disappointment, my friends encouraged me to keep on praying. For several intense days, we were on the phone, sharing news of Harold's progress. His life hung in the balance, and we were not going to let go. We continued to pray the "prayer of faith," imagining Harold well and thanking God that that would happen. As the doctors performed a delicate operation to relieve the pressure from his brain, we prayed that the operation would be a success. We pictured his faculties being restored and imagined him sitting up in bed as we had seen him before, cheerful and effusive.

The operation *was* a success. Gradually Harold got better. In a week, we didn't see him sitting up in bed. We saw him walking down the hallway to greet us! We visited him several times. The last time we dropped in, we were surprised to find his bed empty and made up. I felt a stab of panic. Had Harold suddenly taken a turn for the worse? Was he . . . ? The nurse smiled and assured us that Harold was completely recovered and had gone home sooner than expected.

That was a dramatic moment for me. I remembered Jesus' words: "Take up your bed and walk." It was as if that was exactly what Harold had done. I kept staring at his empty bed. I had a more realistic idea now of how God healed—it took time and often involved a roller coaster of ups and downs; a steady commitment was needed and sometimes it called for sharing deeply in another's suffering; spiritual healing often worked hand in hand with natural and human means of healing (ie. medical). Even though I understood all this, it did not lessen my amazement that God had been there in that hospital room and I saw with the eyes of faith something I had never seen before.

HEALING THE BODY

Once I became convinced that God *can* and *does* heal today, I began to pray for physical healing for myself, my family, and friends. I did this in small ways that came naturally. If my daughter was sick, I placed my hand on her forehead and asked the love of Jesus to flow into her body, filling her with His light and life, and resting her in His perfect peace. Even after the sickness was waning, she would beg for me to put my hand on her forehead and pray because she said, "it felt so good." I've found that even though I experience varying degrees of success with healing prayer, the person being prayed for always feels loved and cared for—which can be healing in itself!

Even though we may say the words and lay our hand on the hurting one, it is Jesus' love flowing through us that heals. So it is not necessary to actually be in physical contact with a person to offer this kind of prayer. Just a couple of days ago I prayed over the phone with a friend who had the flu. I invited Jesus to be right there in her bedroom with her and put a loving hand on her forehead, just as I had done for my daughter. "As soon as you prayed," said my friend, "I felt the pain lift." Not everyone I pray for responds so quickly! But I have discovered, and you will too, that the more often you pray for people, the more often prayer is answered. This is the biblical principle of sowing and reaping: "Whoever sows sparingly will also reap sparingly, and whoever sows generously will also reap generously" (2 Cor. 9:6 NIV). So pray often. You will be surprised what God can do through you.

To receive healing for ourselves or others, I find it helpful to remember that God heals through faith, touch and the Word. Let's look at these three aspects closer.

FAITH

"Daughter, your faith has healed you," said Jesus to the woman who believed that if she only touched Jesus' garment, she would be healed (Luke 8:48 NIV). A Roman centurion believed that Jesus' authority over sickness was so great that He only had to say the word and his servant would be healed. Jesus was amazed by the man's faith and immediately healed his servant. Conversely, Jesus performed very little healing in his home town because of the lack of faith there (Matthew 13:58).

Faith creates a receptive atmosphere for healing. It is good to begin a prayer of healing with an attitude of thankfulness, acknowledging God's love for us and His power to heal. Our own faith can be increased significantly when we add it to the faith of others because Jesus promised: "If two of you on earth agree about anything you ask for, it will be done for you by my Father in heaven" (Matthew 18:19 NIV). I have great faith that God can heal other people, but my faith is lowest when I'm praying for myself. Sickness and pain can be overwhelming and drag us down. That's when I pick up the phone and call a friend, or several, and ask them to pray for me. I may experience some healing then or receive the gift of patience or encouragement until complete healing does come in God's time.

TOUCH

Touch is an important aspect of healing too. As we mentioned earlier, Jesus' most common method of healing was to lay hands on the sick. Physical touch is valuable as an outward sign of our caring and nurture; most people receive it gladly. But in healing prayer, touch also provides a conduit through which God's healing power flows. It is not uncommon to feel a gentle warmth or tingling sensation in the hands as you pray for someone. This doesn't always happen. But it does sometimes, which uggests that prayerful touch actually enhances the healing process as God's life-giving energy is imparted to the person receiving prayer.

When praying for a serious or long-term illness, one of the most useful tools I have learned to use is "soaking prayer," a method whereby someone lays hands on another person repeatedly over an extended period of time, soaking him in God's love.

I have a friend whose seven-year-old son broke his leg. As it healed, X-rays revealed that a bone cyst, a hollow part in the bone, was still evident. If that empty space did not fill in over time, my friend was told that her son would have to have surgery. In most cases, spontaneous healing did not occur. My friend prayed a short soaking prayer every night for three months laying her hands on the broken bone as her son slept. As God had created something out of nothing in Genesis, she imagined His creative power filling in the void in the bone with new healthy tissue. Several months later she was delighted to learn that her prayers had been answered. The bone had begun to fill in and surgery wasn't necessary.

GOD'S WORD

Another powerful tool which is helpful in praying for healing is God's Word (Psalm 107:20). This is particularly true when there are underlying causes to physical illness. Doctors tell us that perhaps eighty percent of sickness is psychosomatic, or psychologically related.

Scripture, says Paul, can penetrate beneath the surface of who we are and uncover what is lodged in our innermost being. "The word of God is living and powerful, and sharper than any two-edged sword, piercing even to the division of soul and spirit, and of joints and marrow, and is a discerner of the thoughts and intents of the heart" (Hebrews 4:12). If anxiety leads to an ulcer, God's Word will reveal that and encourage us to resolve whatever is causing the anxiety; if arthritis, a stiffening of the joints, is rooted in an unhealthy need to control people and things around us, God's Word will lay that bare and motivate us to deal with it.

My friend, Christine, asked me to pray with her about a debilitating pain in her neck. The pain was lodged in the cervical portion of her spine, the point at which the neck and back join. I asked Christine what was going on in her life. She was under a lot of stress, facing the possible loss of her job and her house and some close friends, which she called a "heart problem." She was also shouldering a great deal of work at church. As I prayed with her, a phrase from Scripture came to mind: "The Lord lifts up those who are bowed down" (Psalm 146:8 NIV). Those words also formed a picture in my mind of Christine as a lovely flower bent down by an invisible weight at the "neck" of the stem. The invisible weight was made up of hidden burdens Christine was carrying: anger, self-pity, a false sense of responsibility. As these were released one by one, Christine would be free to stand up in full health and strength again.

This is what happened. Continuing to work with her physical therapist on the physical problem, Christine and I also worked together in prayer on the emotional and spiritual dimensions of the problem. This involved healing of hurt, confession of her own sinful responses, eg. resentment and anger, forgiveness to resolve relational conflicts, and practical steps such as cutting back on commitments at church.

HEALING THE WHOLE PERSON

It is important to say here that the parts of our make-up are so closely intertwined, it is sometimes hard to tell whether sickness is physical, emotional or spiritual. Often all three aspects are involved. Jesus knew this. This is why His healings were often multifaceted. We learn to recognize this, too: the same Holy Spirit who led Jesus leads us. By focusing intently on the person in need with one ear, as Jesus did, and with the other on the Holy Spirit, my first question when praying for someone or myself is, "Lord, what particular aspect of this problem do you want to heal at this moment?"

God is sovereign. He may choose to heal one part of a problem or several aspects at one time. He may choose to take away physical pain, or touch a deep emotional wound, or set us free from an unseen spiritual hold that evil has on our lives. In this chapter we discussed how God heals physical sickness, but so much of human hurt is emotional and spiritual in nature that a great deal of healing the whole person also involves healing the heart. We'll explore that in the next chapter.

But first, let's come into the presence of Jesus through prayer. We'll come needy this time, bringing our aches and pains, our weaknesses, our hidden crippledness. We'll come this time not even with an ounce of strength, but rather borne along by the strength of others.

THE GIFT
OF HEALING

R *ead and Reflect*
on Mark 2:3–12 (TLB)

Four men arrived carrying a paralyzed man on a stretcher. They couldn't get to Jesus through the crowd, so they dug through the clay roof above his head and lowered the sick man on his stretcher, right down in front of Jesus. When Jesus saw how strongly they believed that he would help, Jesus said to the sick man, "Son, your sins are forgiven!"

But some of the Jewish religious leaders said to themselves as they sat there, "What? This is blasphemy! Does He think he is God? For only God can forgive sins."

Jesus could read their minds and said to them at once, "Why does this bother you? I, the Messiah, have the authority on earth to forgive sins. But talk is cheap—anybody could say that. So I'll prove it to you by healing this man." Then, turning to the paralyzed man, he commanded, "Pick up your stretcher and go on home, for you are healed!"

The man jumped up, took the stretcher, and pushed his way through the stunned onlookers! Then how they praised God. "We've never seen anything like this before!" they exclaimed.

Imagine yourself as the paralyzed man in this story. You are flat on your back, unable to move. You've been sick a long time. Friends ask you from time to time how you're doing. You don't want to bore them with the details. The bottom line is, after endless tests, the doctors still don't know what's wrong. How can you share with anyone your frustration, dread, and anger? "I try not to think about it," you tell your friends with a weak smile.

Now your friends have come to you. Jesus is in town, they say. Jesus. Yes, you've heard of Jesus. Everyone has heard of Jesus. A faith healer. Your friends are convinced that if they can get you to see Jesus, you'll be healed. They seem so sure. You sigh. You don't want to put them to the trouble. You don't want to be a burden.

But your friends insist. Their faces are bright with hope. They are so sure that Jesus can make you well that you begin to believe it yourself. One of them squeezes your hand to give you courage.

Soon you are on the move, carried forward by your faith-filled friends. Your friends are enthusiastic, energetic, but gradually the pace slows. There are obstacles. The crowd is much bigger than they imagined. How can they get through to Jesus? Perhaps they should turn back, you suggest. But as one person's faith sags, another's surges. The roof! And up you go. Slowly, steadily, they mount the steps, then put down the stretcher. Unbelievable. Now they are on their hands and knees digging.

You are lifted once more, then carefully lowered through the roof of the house where Jesus is teaching. Little by little, the stretcher is let down with ropes. The crowd is stunned. Jesus steps forward, raising his hand to hush the murmurs and whispers. Everyone stands back.

Jesus looks up at your friends and smiles, acknowledging their faith. He doesn't seem to be offended that this unexpected event has stopped the meeting. He looks at you. His gaze is tender, but penetrating. He seems to know in a glance everything that is hidden in your heart—the inner paralysis that other people cannot see. The pride, the self-pity, the sense of unworthiness, the lack of faith. Are there other weaknesses that cripple you?

Jesus says, "_____ (insert your name), your sins are forgiven."

This statement angers the religious leaders in the room. You hear the intensity of their voices, but you are so aware of the intensity in your heart, that their discourse sounds far away. As soon as Jesus pronounced those words of forgiveness, you felt released, freed in some way, as if invisible shackles on your heart have been sprung open.

This is remarkable enough. But now Jesus says to His detractors that He not only has the power to forgive sin and heal hearts, but He also has the power to heal bodies. Jesus turns to you and says: *Get up, take your stretcher and go home.* Even as Jesus speaks the command, you can feel a wave of warmth traveling down you body, loosening the stiff joints and muscles in your thighs, your legs, your toes. Before you realize what's happening, you're actually on your feet. You're incredulous. It's like receiving a gift you don't deserve. "Take it," Jesus seems to intimate. "It's yours."

And you do take it. You jump for joy! You smile at Jesus, then glance up at your friends. The hole in the roof frames their faces. One is beaming. Another is tear-stained. One lets out a loud shout. Like that hole in the roof, your faith, once so limited, has been ripped open too, and with your friend you want to shout it to the world.

Oh, how incredible love is! How incredible! Hoping, faltering, persisting, searching, love made a way that day. Love made a way.

THE GIFT
OF INNER HEALING

"He has sent Me to heal the brokenhearted."
—*Isaiah 61:1*

*W*hen Jesus was asked what the greatest commandment was, He answered: "You shall love the Lord your God with all your heart, with all your soul, with all your strength, and with all your mind," and "your neighbor as yourself" (Luke 10:27). To illustrate how we should love others, He told the story of the Good Samaritan.

You know the story. An unfortunate traveler "falls into the hands of robbers." He is stripped naked, beaten and left half dead by the side of the road. Two passers-by see the injured man, but continue on their way. A third traveler sees the man and responds with compassion. The Samaritan has places to go and people to see too, but he decides to stop and help. He draws close to the injured man, kneels down beside him and tends his wounds. Then he puts the man on his donkey, while he walks, and takes him to an inn where he can fully recover.

Jesus said that's how we are to love others—with the same

care and compassion that the Samaritan showed this man in need. Of course, we are not accustomed to seeing people beaten up and left for dead by the side of the freeway as we travel to the office, take the kids to school, or buzz around town on errands. But if we slow down just long enough to take a good look at those around us, we will see people every day who are beaten up and bruised by life. Brokenhearted. Hurting. Carrying secret burdens, secret pain.

I believe that Jesus is suggesting by this story that we are to be just as attentive to the inner wounds of people as we are to their physical woundedness. Healing heart hurts is sometimes called "inner healing" because emotional and spiritual hurts are not readily visible as physical problems are. These wounds are hidden, but they are very real.

Jesus was sent, and He sends us to bind up the wounds of the brokenhearted. He invites us to come alongside Him to do this tender work, first being sensitive to the need, then drawing close with compassion, and, little by little, learning to tend the inner wounds of the heart. It may be that professional help is needed for full recovery—perhaps it will be our role to help someone find that kind of help, as the Samaritan took the injured man to the inn—but there is much that you and I can do along the highways and byways of life to offer Jesus' love to someone who is hurting.

It's wonderful to learn the special way Jesus ministers inner healing not only so we can help others, but also because we need to be attentive to our own inner wounds. There are many times when I've felt bruised and battered by life. Do I stop and help myself? Often not. I don't deal with grievance; I swallow anger; I deny hurt. In this chapter we'll explore ways that we can come to Jesus in prayer to receive healing for our own brokenness as well as learning to help others.

BEING PRESENT IN PAIN

"The Lord is near to those who have a broken heart," the psalmist testified in gratitude (Psalm 34:18). When someone is in pain, Jesus draws close. Sometimes He uses our hands, our voice, our ears to do that. I have a friend who had been away from church for decades when she decided to return. She had no idea that Sunday morning that she would be so moved by the experience: she just hung her head and cried and cried. Without saying a word, someone who sensed her inner pain reached out a hand and took hold of hers. My friend was grateful.

She couldn't even put into words what she felt. Feeling the heartbreak of living alone all those years without God, she was deeply aware of her sin and unworthiness and even more aware of God's overwhelming love and acceptance. As she struggled with the depths of who she was and the depths of who God was, that warm hand continued to sustain and encourage her. It was as if that hand was an extension of God's love offered especially to her. My friend was so overcome with tears she wasn't even able to thank the woman whose touch had meant so much. A small gesture, but a life-changing one. It was that extended hand that drew my friend back into the Body of Christ.

I have another friend whose warm voice on the telephone sustains me when I am feeling heartbroken. Last year I had to fly to Texas to be close to my mother-in-law, who was dying of a terminal disease. I felt overwhelmed. Would I be able to say the right thing, do the right thing? My friend listened patiently and said simply, "Just be yourself." That little phrase released me to face a fearful situation unafraid.

Another way we can be present to each other in pain is simply to listen. "The road to the heart," wrote Voltaire, "is the ear." Psychologists tell us that just the act of listening to someone in pain is therapeutic. Often when we talk a problem out, issues become clearer and solutions apparent. But even more important than finding solutions to problems, a sympathetic ear shows someone you care. A friend called me recently, barely able to talk through tears, spilling out a complex problem I could never solve. "I feel so much better," she said, after I had offered nothing more than a listening ear. "You don't have to fix it. It just helps to know that someone else understands."

Caring touch, words of encouragement, a listening ear—these are the simple everyday tools of inner healing. There are more complex tools which we can learn on the job as we stretch ourselves, but these are the basics.

INNER HEALING PRAYER

You may already be sensitive to the heart cries of those around you and find yourself moved by the impulse of God's love to draw close to people in pain. But beyond that, you are not sure how to really help. How do we bind up the wounds of the brokenhearted?

Just as the Samaritan had something in hand—wine and oil—we have something in hand—prayer. Prayer is the way God pours out His healing upon a deeply wounded heart.

It can be very simple. Let me give you an example of how powerful a single word in prayer can be. I once prayed for a woman from Latin America. She was the tenth of ten children; she grew up knowing she was unwanted, a burden to her mother. She had married early to escape an unhappy home situation. Twenty years and two children later, uprooted from her own country, she was in deep distress because her husband now wanted a divorce. Unwanted as a child, now as a wife, she felt forsaken, devastated.

As I listened to her story, a verse of Scripture came to mind: "His loved ones are very *precious* and He does not lightly let them die" (Psalm 116:15 TLB italics added). I had a clear sense that God wanted to impress the word "precious" into the heart of this woman who felt so unloved, because she was still deeply loved by Him. Very gently, I traced my fingertips over her forehead, the center of her emotions and thinking, and spoke that word, "precious." Maria smiled.

Then it occurred to me that God wanted that special word from Him to go deeper. I asked Maria, "How do you say 'precious' in Spanish?"

"Preciosa."

Again, I touched her forehead and pronounced the same word, this time in her native language. Her response was remarkable. It was as if that word flowed like a healing balm over the open wound of her heart. Her face, at first darkened with worry, became radiant. For one so fragile, so crushed underfoot, receiving that word of high worth was a wondrous gift. To know we are loved, truly loved, is the most important word of healing any of us will ever hear—in any language.

Whenever I pray for inner healing for someone else or receive the gift of God's love spoken to me in prayer, I am always struck by how deeply personal this kind of prayer is.

God knows and appreciates who each of us is: our background, our make-up, our most private thoughts and feelings. He can speak to our emotions and spirits as well as to our minds, using pictures, dreams, impressions, as well as words.

Precious. In a thousand ways, God longs to tell us how precious we are to him, especially when we're hurting. Yesterday I was feeling crushed, literally bruised and beaten up. "The Lord is my shepherd," I began to read the twenty-third psalm. When I got to the phrase, "he restores my soul," I just lingered there. Those were God's words meant for me in that moment. In prayer, I saw myself as a helpless little lamb, so crippled I couldn't even struggle to my feet. Jesus knelt down, picked me up in his Shepherd's arms and held me close. Slowly the shattered pieces of my heart began to come back together again.

THE HEALING POWER OF JESUS

We learn to bind up the wounds of the brokenhearted by letting Jesus tend our wounds and pour out His love lavishly on us. Then when we are sent to bind up the wounds of someone else, we humbly know that we go not in our own strength or even by our own leading, but in His name and by His leading. We ask ourselves, "What would He do? What would He say to heal a hurting heart?"

One of the most remarkable ways I've seen Jesus heal inner wounds is memory healing, a specific kind of healing prayer. If you remember, I described how I first experienced this myself in chapter two. Jesus came gently into a devastating memory and expressed His love to me at a point of utter humiliation when I was thirteen. His love not only healed the emotional pain of that memory, but it also healed my broken self-esteem in such a way that I became a much more confident adult.

Most of us aren't aware of how much control our memories have over us. I certainly wasn't. Of course, psychologists and counselors know this. They tell us that many emotional problems that have a strong hold on us—uncontrollable anger, compulsive fears and anxieties, a sense of worthlessness that we just can't shake—are often caused by patterns built up from past hurts. Even though they can help us look at the past and uncover the roots of this behavior, many times they cannot offer real healing.

I have a friend who went to a counselor, but stopped going because she "wasn't getting anywhere." She discovered that her parents had done her untold damage as a child. This revelation just brought anger. Because there was no avenue to resolve these feelings, she went away feeling worse than when she'd come. Understanding by itself cannot bring healing.

I do not deny the good that counseling can do. Certainly there are great benefits to be gained from understanding ourselves and why we are the way we are. But I have found that the healing power of Jesus as experienced through prayer can add a powerful dimension to transforming our past in such a way that we can live life in the present in a whole new way. How are hurtful memories healed through prayer?

HEALING HURTFUL MEMORIES

Think of your life as a house. How comfortable and relaxing to spend time in the large, spacious living room or in the sunny family room. However, all of the rooms in your house are not filled with laughter. There are other rooms—dark inner places, cellars, closets, empty, isolated places. Sad places. These are where your hurtful memories hide. Jesus longs to bring the light of His presence into *every* room in your life, to set you free in *every* area of your life.

There are many rooms in our lives that haven't been opened for years. We are afraid to open them again. However, with Love beside us there is no place we cannot go. So in memory-healing prayer, we are gently guided back to a painful time in life, often to a childhood memory which may be the source of inner wounds that still cause damage in adulthood. In prayer, a particular scene is relived, except it is revisited in a different way. This time Jesus is invited into the scene, into the secret room of hurt, and something wonderful happens. His loving presence brings a warmth and light into the darkness of that memory that fundamentally transforms it.

How does the healing miracle occur? The facts of the memory remain the same: the incident happened and that can't be undone, but the painful feelings associated with the memory, which still have power over us, can be released through prayer. When the suffering Christ enters into our suffering, it's as if His love absorbs all the poison of that moment and it can no longer spill out into the rest of our lives. "By His wounds we are healed" (Isaiah 53:5 NIV).

You may want to try memory-healing prayer yourself or ask a close and trusted friend, who is also close to the Lord, to pray with you. Or, you can pray for your friend. Some cases may require the help of someone more experienced in inner-healing prayer, but for the most part this kind of prayer can be accessible to us all.

The first step in memory healing is to choose a memory that Jesus wants to enter into at the moment. This requires the help of the Holy Spirit. The Holy Spirit is God's appointed Counselor and thoroughly knows us: He can search our minds and hearts and pinpoint a critical hurt that needs healing. So begin in prayer, just waiting, just listening, and ask Him to bring to mind what He wants to deal with. As a doctor first diagnoses a problem before treating it, in prayer spiritual discernment is used to reveal the cause of inner woundedness.

Questions can be helpful. If someone is feeling intense shame, I ask, "When did you first feel this way?" Basic questions about someone's background can also help identify hurtful incidents or painful relationships. Did you have a happy childhood? Did you feel loved? What was your relationship with your mom like? Your dad? A traumatic incident may come to mind immediately, eg. sexual abuse or domestic violence, but often a seemingly small, insignificant event can still cause much pain. Feeling humiliated in school, being left out of a family gathering, a parent flying into a rage over a child's mistake can leave deep emotional scars.

(Hurtful memories aren't always childhood memories, but if you are trying to get to the root of a problem, in the majority of cases, they will be. Children are so open and vulnerable, so defenseless to hurt, that deep, delibating pain is often lodged in the experience of these tender years).

Once a memory comes to mind, the next step is to enter into that memory in prayer. If I am praying with someone, I ask Jesus the Good Shepherd to take hold of that person's hand and guide us safely back to that moment. Then I ask the person to recall as vividly as possible the scene of the memory. What time of day is it? Which room in the house are you in? If someone else is in the memory (often a family member or friend), you can ask about their facial expressions, tone of voice, etc.

The third step in memory healing is to picture (with the eyes of faith) Jesus actually being there. Most people find this surprisingly easy to do; some cannot see Him at first, but can sense His presence. You then ask, "Where is He? What is He doing?" As the incident unfolds, Jesus enters the scene and does what Love would do to heal the emotional pain of the situation. He might play ball or fly a kite with a little boy whose father never had time for him; He might tenderly put his arms around a little girl who is cowering in the corner witnessing domestic violence and carry her out of the room to safety.

This may appear to be psychological manipulation, but it is

not. Scripture says that when two or three are gathered together, Jesus is there too. Inner-healing prayer simply invites Jesus to be present in prayer in an active way. I also believe that this kind of prayer experience is more than psychological manipulation because its effects bring real change in attitudes and actions.

THE RE-MAKING OF A MEMORY

Let me give you an example of memory healing. I once prayed for a woman who had lived for a long time with deep anger. Anger was poisoning all of Diane's relationships, including her relationship with God. "My walk with God is dead," she said sadly. "I want to grow in the Lord, but I've stopped." Diane wanted desperately to rid herself of this anger, but how?

In prayer, we asked the Holy Spirit to reveal the source of this anger. A devastating memory surfaced in Diane's mind. It was so painful to her that she told me later she felt nauseated and wanted to vomit just remembering it. What was this revolting memory?

To anybody else, it probably would not appear to be that traumatic, but remembrances are personal things. Only each of us knows how much pain is hidden behind the locked door of a repressed memory.

Diane described the memory, picturing herself as a ten-year-old dashing downstairs to school. That day she had decided to wear her sister's orange skirt that everyone said made her sister look so cute. Diane felt like a million dollars. As Diane skipped downstairs, she saw her mother standing at the bottom of the stairs. "You can't wear *that!*" she shouted. "It makes you look fat and ugly!" Diane's fragile self-esteem was crushed. She hated her mother at that moment.

Diane struggled with anger and hatred toward her mother all her life. The "orange skirt incident" was one memory of many that locked those feelings into her heart and also contributed to feelings of self-hate that led her later into alcoholism and over-eating. Diane had always seen herself as her mother had seen her that morning: fat and ugly.

In prayer, we relived that moment, but this time invited Jesus to be present in the memory. When Diane as a little girl went to the top of the stairs and looked down, she saw Jesus standing between her and her mother. Instead of seeing her mother's scolding eyes, she saw Jesus looking up at her with love. Rather than hearing her mother's bitter words, she heard Jesus speaking words of endearment: "You look wonderful today, honey." With a smile, He gathered her up in his arms and took her to an easy chair in the living room, where she sat in His lap and read stories before going to school.

The prayer could have ended there. But God wanted to heal more than Diane's childhood hurt that morning. He also wanted to begin to heal her relationship with her mother. To do this, Diane needed to see her mother with new eyes. As our prayer continued, the scene of Diane sitting in Jesus' lap in her living room changed to the biblical scene of Diane sitting in Jesus' lap under the tree as He blessed the children (the interactive prayer we used in chapter two). Sitting in Jesus' lap, Diane felt loved and cared for; then I asked her if she could imagine her mother as a little girl there too.

This was startling to Diane. It seemed strange at first to think of her mom as a child, but there she was: dressed in the same pink-checked pinafore that she dressed her own daughter in now. Diane suddenly had a whole new insight into her mother. "I remembered that my mom was once a little girl whose mother had been cold and unapproving." Diane's mother had treated her as she had been treated as a child. Understanding where her mother's anger came from, Diane realized that underneath her mom's brusque exterior was a hurting little girl who needed Jesus' love just as much as she did.

For the first time, Diane felt compassion for her mother. This freed her to let go of her anger and forgive her because, as she said, "My grandmother was a bitter old woman and my mom's become bitter too. Not me! I know I can only guarantee this by forgiving my mom. Unforgiveness and anger only eat away at the happy things in your life."

Some weeks later, Diane wrote me: "I've been able to speak with my mom since the retreat. *No anger!* We're going to spend a weekend together this summer." Once Diane had let go her long-held anger, her relationship with her mom changed dramatically. Also, to her surprise, she began to feel an incredible compassion for other people—"I'm not numb anymore"—and her relationship with God became more alive than ever.

THE CLEANSING POWER OF JESUS

"Love is a many-splendored thing," and so is healing. Diane's healing moment set her free in several ways. First, she received the love of Jesus, which healed her own hurt; then she looked beyond her hurt to see her mother's pain, allowing forgiveness to let love flow between them again. Finally, she began to see how harbored anger led to bitterness which caused self-inflicted wounds. "The man who broods over a wrong poisons his own soul," writes David Augsburger.[1]

No matter how much we have been hurt, we are still responsible for our own reactions to that hurt. If we choose to hold on to anger, resentment, and bitterness, sometimes our sinful responses actually cause us more pain than the original hurt. The

Bible warns us not to let a "root of bitterness" spring up in our hearts because it will "defile" us (Hebrews 12:15).

Few of us realize how serious sin is. I once heard sin described vividly in terms I finally understood. A pastor, who had taught about the subject all his life, suddenly saw how deadly sin was when he came face to face with a cancerous growth that was taken out of his wife. Left alone in the laboratory after his wife's surgery, he looked at the ugly tumor and felt a rage well up inside him. "I wanted to club it and club it and club it because of what it had done to my wife. Slowly, surely, silently it had drawn the life out of her," he said.

"Sin is like that," he continued. "It is a living organism that sucks life out of us. It does something to us. It drains our enthusiasm, drains our love for the Lord. It drains us of energy and strength to do His work, and makes us lifeless."[2]

How can the destructive growth of sin be stopped? Repentance. Just as a surgeon can stop cancer by cutting out a tumor (the source of the disease), inner healing comes when a Christian acknowledges and confesses sin. "Therefore," Scripture says, "confess your sins to each other and pray for each other so that you may be healed" (James 5:16, NIV).

Another very important aspect of inner-healing prayer is applying the cleansing power of Jesus to heart hurts. This means helping the person receiving prayer to recognize and take responsiblity for her own sin in a hurtful situation because, even though we are not aware of it, there is much that we do ourselves to nourish and feed our own pain. In my experience, I've seen that inner-healing prayer often progresses in stages: first the immediate hurt is addressed, then it is as if a defensive outer layer of pain is peeled back and the wounded heart is more open to let prayer go deeper. This often involves the conviction of the Holy Spirit that one's own sin is a part of the problem.

In Diane's case, for example, she came to realize that her own unforgiveness and anger caused her as much pain as her mother's emotional abuse. Acknowledging and confessing these sins aloud to God before another Christian brought as much healing to her as the moving memory prayer that came earlier. There is incredible healing power in confessing our sins to one another because they are then brought into the light, where they no longer have any hidden power over us.

Taking responsibility for sin includes naming the sin specifically and asking God's forgiveness. I feel it is important for the person being prayed for to do this aloud in her own words. Sometimes I put out my hands and ask the person to imagine that my hands are the hands of Jesus. Then she puts out her hands on my open palms. I ask, "Is there anything you want to say to Jesus?" This often leads to confession. Then I ask her to imagine letting go of confessed sin and relinquishing it into Jesus' hands.

As a rabbinical reflection states so beautifully: "If a man has an unclean thing in his hands, he may wash them in all the seas of the world, and he will never be clean; but if he throws the unclean thing away, a little water will suffice."

After a person has spoken a confession, I then pronounce words of forgiveness in Jesus' name. "If we confess our sins," I quote 1 John 1:9, "He is faithful and just to forgive us our sins and to cleanse us from *all* unrighteousness" (italics added). I stress the word "all" because the Lord really does forgive us completely and it is wonderfully freeing to know that.

It is good to take a moment to let these words sink in. Just as we often fail to take the time to drink in God's love, we often fail to drink in God's forgiveness fully, to let the cleansing power of Jesus flow over us and wash away the filthiness of sin, the dirty feelings of failure, because, in Jesus' love and purity, we are made holy even as He is. It is Jesus' blood, His very life, that makes us clean. Grace, as the old hymn says, is amazing.

THE AUTHORITATIVE POWER OF JESUS

We have seen how the healing power of Jesus can minister to the hurts that have been done to us and how the cleansing power of Jesus can free us from the way we hurt ourselves. But there is still another dimension to healing inner wounds that we need to touch on—the spiritual dimension. This requires deliverance, another kind of prayer method grounded in the authoritative power of Jesus.

In the last chapter, I said that Jesus came to set people free from the powers of darkness that oppressed them. If you've been sick, you know how heavy and dark physical illness feels. If you've ever struggled with an emotional problem, like depression, you know how oppressive that can be. In the same way, evil can lodge in our hearts and oppress our spirits. Because the spiritual side of our make-up affects every other aspect of who we are, this may be a factor in any kind of suffering.

As we mature as Christians, Paul says, we should train ourselves to distinguish good from evil (Hebrews 5:14). There are two reasons for this. The first is for our own protection: we need to recognize the darkness in our own hearts so that we will not be deceived by it. Also, as lightbearers for Christ, we are called to bring His healing light into situations of darkness, wherever that may be.

For me, these situations have come as I've engaged the pain in people's lives while praying for inner healing. Plumbing the depths of someone's heart to discern some underlying source of hurt, sometimes I would find that prayer was hindered by hitting hard, resistant places that God's Spirit could not penetrate.

These, I discovered, were places where Satan had a foothold in a person's life.

According to the *American Heritage Dictionary*, a *foothold* is "a firm or secure position enabling one to proceed with confidence; especially, a secure military base." In Ephesians 4:26–27, Paul warns us not to let Satan get a "foothold" in our lives by letting anger fester. Sin which is cherished and sustained becomes deeply-entrenched and gives the devil a firm base of operations to control our hearts and minds.

Relieving the pain and destruction in someone's life often requires "rooting out" this kind of evil presence. It cannot be loved away; it cannot be confessed away. It must be cast out by the authority of Jesus. Jesus gave His disciples authority "over all the power of the enemy" (Luke 10:19). This is when that authority is needed.

Before someone is prayed for in this way, the spiritual forces that are present need to be clearly and carefully identified. To do this takes a gift from the Holy Spirit called "discerning of spirits" (1 Corinthians 12:10). Once an evil spirit is named, a gentle, but firm deliverance prayer is used to command it to leave—*always* in the name of Jesus. We do not have any authority in ourselves to overcome evil, but Jesus does. So we say, "I command you, spirit of rejection, in the name of Jesus to depart." Then the Holy Spirit is invited to fill in the empty space in the person's heart with His love and power and whatever was missing, in this case acceptance.

I am amazed by what this prayer can do. As people are released from these oppressive spirits, they physically look more relaxed, softer and freer, loosened up as if invisible logjams in their personalities have been dislodged. If these blockages have hindered inner-healing prayer, it is now free to proceed unimpeded.

Even though deliverance prayer can be very effective when it's called for, I want to mention a word of caution. Deliverance prayer is just one of many prayer approaches; it is a specialized tool to be used in conjunction with other prayer methods. In the majority of cases, it is considered only as a last resort. It is also not a "quick fix," a prayer that easily "exorcises" someone's problems. Even though problems can be uprooted by prayer, lasting change only comes as new positive habit patterns replace old unhealthy ones and a person grows stronger in health and wholeness through regular spiritual disciplines such as prayer, Bible study, and involvement in a Christian community.

BECOMING AN OVERCOMER

"In this world you will have trouble," said Jesus. "But take heart! I have overcome the world" (John 16:33 NIV). With Jesus' help, He promises we can overcome the world too (1 John 5:4–5). In this chapter I've shared specific ways in prayer that Jesus can bring healing to broken hearts. As we grow in prayer, we can use these methods to overcome trouble in our own lives.

When emotional hurt comes my way, I have learned to use memory healing to revisit the scene right away with Jesus (the hurtful incident might have happened as recently as the day before). "Lord, why did I feel so deeply hurt?" I ask Jesus. "Why did I overreact?" In prayer, He might reveal that the incident "echoes" from pain in the past. A specific memory may come to mind that still needs healing.

Next I ask, "How did I contribute to the problem? Is there some hidden sin on my part?" If so, I confess that to the Lord, repenting of anger and asking His Spirit to fill me with compassion and patience; repenting of pride and asking for His humility; repenting of self-pity and asking for His joy.

If I have repented and repented of this sin and it still persists, I assume that there might be a spiritual cause. I confess the sin, repent of it and take authority over it in Jesus' name. For example, if fear is a problem, I pray, "In the name of Jesus, I rebuke you, spirit of fear, because scripture says that 'God has not given us a spirit of fear, but of power and of love and of a sound mind'" (2 Timothy 1:7).

If you have a particular weakness, it is good to memorize a Bible verse that counters that weakness. The Bible instructs us to come against Satan with God's Word, "the sword of the Spirit," the offensive weapon Christians are encouraged to use in spiritual warfare (Ephesians 6:17). Jesus used scripture to resist the devil when He was tempted (Matthew 4:1–11), and you can resist evil in the same way (James 4:7).

The best way to protect yourself from the encroachment of evil—which we are all vulnerable to—is to "walk in the light." "God is light; and in Him there is no darkness at all," writes John, who encourages us to walk so close to Jesus that we know immediately when we have offended Him or other people. Living a life of transparency, we are quick to confess, quick to restore broken relationships.

"But if anybody does sin," says John, the beloved disciple who was so understanding of human frailty, "we have one who speaks to the Father in our defense—Jesus Christ, the Righteous One" (1 John 2:1 NIV). Jesus is our advocate, our healer, our redeemer.

THE GENTLE HEALER

Jesus is a gentle healer. Scripture says that He is close to the brokenhearted, and He lifts up those who are bowed down. There are so many times that we find ourselves bruised and beaten up by the side of the road. Caught in life's circumstances, victimized by others, sometimes victims of our own transgressions, we fall into the hands of "robbers"—sin, hurt, evil. We are robbed of peace and joy, robbed of happiness, of wholeness. Where can we go but to Jesus?

In prayer, let's come into His presence now and receive the gift of inner healing.

THE GIFT
OF INNER HEALING

 *ead and Reflect
on John 8:3–11*

Then the scribes and the Pharisees brought to Him a
woman caught in adultery. And when they had set her in the midst,
they said to Him, "Teacher, this woman was caught in adultery, in the
very act. Now Moses, in the law, commanded us that such should be
stoned. But what do You say?" This they said, testing Him, that they
might have something of which to accuse Him. But Jesus stooped
down and wrote on the ground with His finger, as though He did not
hear.

So when they continued asking Him, He raised Himself up and
said to them, "He who is without sin among you, let him throw a
stone at her first." And again He stooped down and wrote on the
ground. Then those who heard it, being convicted by their con-
science, went out one by one, beginning with the oldest even to the
last. And Jesus was left alone, and the woman standing in the midst.
When Jesus had raised Himself up and saw no one but the woman,
He said to her, "Woman, where are those accusers of yours? Has no
one condemned you?"

She said, "No one, Lord."

And Jesus said to her, "Neither do I condemn you; go and sin no
more."

"Guilty!" cries the crowd, and they take up stones. The
woman has no defender. Caught in the act, dragged naked out
of the bedroom, a cloak thown quickly around her shoulders to

keep out the cold. But it cannot hide her sin. Picture yourself as that woman—humiliated, terrified.

You are thrust in front of your neighbors, townspeople, people you know. You feel so ashamed. They look at you with disdain. You feel like a small child battered by the condemning look of an accusing parent. You want to run and hide, but where can you go?

Even your own heart condemns you. "Guilty!" it points a finger. A sharp stab of pain cuts at the core of who you are. Overwhelmed by waves of sadness and shame, you sink to the ground, huddled in a heap.

The crowd presses in. They tower over you, not only bearing down on you but also on Jesus, the one they are questioning. Instead of answering their question, He bends down and writes in the dust. There is a stillness about Him, a composure that will not be hurried. He glances up at you. His eyes are not like the others; they are soft with mercy.

Then He speaks to the crowd with a voice sure and steady, with authority. There is silence. A long silence . . . Now *their* heads are bowed. *Thud.* A hard rock hits the ground. *Thud. Thud.* Another, then another. One by one, your accusers walk away.

You are left alone with Jesus. Quietly, He comes close. He reaches out and lifts your chin up with His hand. He smiles and wipes away the tears that stain your cheeks. His touch takes your breath away. He makes you feel cherished. Lovely.

Slowly, He helps you to your feet.

"Go now," He says, "and live life differently."

Yes, you feel your shoulders straighten, you will. His touch, so tender, brings back a forgotten memory: as a child, you remember cupping a wounded bird with a broken wing in your hands. You wanted so badly to mend it and let it fly free. Suddenly, you realize that *you are that bird*, wounded, restored, set free.

"Today is the first day of the rest of your life"—and you're going to live it in a whole new way.

THE GIFT
OF FORGIVENESS

"As the Lord has forgiven you, so you also must for-
give."

—Colossians 3:13 (RSV)

*I*n the biblical story that ends the previous chapter, we feel
compassion for the adulteress who is about to be stoned by
an angry crowd. Eager to bare our good hearts, we are quick to
sympathize with the victim in the story. But if we're honest, we
must confess that we've often chosen another role. Probably
more times than we'd care to admit, we've held a rock in hand,
we've judged, we've condemned, and not always shown mercy
as we should.

According to John's account of this moving story, Jesus bends
down and writes something on the ground with his finger. No
one knows what He wrote. Scholars all have their theories, but
my guess is that Jesus wrote a single word: FORGIVE.

Of all of Jesus' commands, this is probably the one we wres-
tle with the most. Could you forgive the adulteress if she were

your neighbor, *your* daughter, the woman who had been un-
faithful with *your* husband? Again and again, we are faced with
difficult situations like this. A friend disappoints us. A child
goes astray. A loved one betrays our trust.

Forgiveness lies at the very heart of healing. "If my years in
the healing ministry have taught me one thing more than another," says Cannon Jim Glennon, a well-known minister of
healing prayer, "it is that nothing contributes more to sickness
than resentment, and more to healing than to forgive . . ."[1]

Even though we mentioned forgiveness in the last chapter, I
want to explore it now in greater depth because it is so central
to all kinds of healing—emotional and spiritual, and often physical. We'll ask hard questions. Why should we forgive? How can
we truly forgive from the heart? How can forgiveness bring healing? Let's begin with the most basic question.

WHAT IS FORGIVENESS?

"Forgiveness is a special kind of love that asks us to remain
open, vulnerable, and caring even though we have been
wounded, offended, hurt or pained," says Doris Donnelly.[2] Forgiveness does not come easily. When we're hurt, our natural
response is to do what the tender anemone does: just as it closes
its arms around itself for protection when attacked, we shut our
hearts and withdraw our affection in response to emotional
pain. Worst of all, we are tempted to avoid the risk of loving
again.

Given our natural tendency to hide from hurt, how can we
remain open in the face of pain? As the old adage says, "To err
is human; to forgive, divine." We can't humanly do it. Everything in us cries out against remaining vulnerable and caring
when we've been wounded. We clench our fists in retaliation or

express our hate in subtler ways—slander, judgment or keeping our distance from the offender. How can we do otherwise? Out of the meager resources of our own hearts, it will always be a struggle to fully forgive life's deepest hurts. But where our resources end, God's begin. "My strength," we are promised, "is made perfect in weakness" (2 Corinthians 12:9). It is at our point of greatest weakness, of utter dependence, that divine love can empower us to do what we could never do on our own.

No story better illustrates this than the story of Corrie ten Boom. You may be familiar with the story. It is a well-known story, but worth retelling again and again. After surviving the atrocities of a Nazi concentration camp, this small, determined woman went back to postwar Germany to help heal the unspeakable pain that still hung heavy over people's lives long after World War II was over. She went from church to church, speaking about God's love and the healing power of forgiveness.

One day as Corrie spoke in a church service, her blood froze. "It was in a church in Munich where I was speaking in 1947 that I saw him," Corrie remembers, "a balding heavyset man in a gray overcoat, a brown felt hat clutched between his hands. One moment I saw the overcoat and the brown hat, the next, a blue uniform and a visored cap with its skull and crossbones."

Memories of the concentration camp where Corrie and her sister Betsy had been tortured, humiliated, and where her sister had died, came flooding back: the mocking men, the heaps of clothing as prisoners were stripped naked, her sister's pain-blanched face. The man at the back of the room had been one of her jailers.

As the church emptied, the man came forward, beaming and bowing. "How grateful I am for your message, Fraulein! To think that, as you say, He has washed my sins away!" During Corrie's talk she had mentioned Ravenstruck, the camp where she had been. He had been there too, he said. Even though Corrie recognized the man, he did not know her: she had just been one of many faceless prisoners. But the former S. S. guard had become a Christian, and he wanted to ask her forgiveness. He held his hand out, "Fraulein, will you forgive me?"

Corrie struggled to raise her hand, but she could not. "I, who had preached so often . . . the need to forgive, kept my hand at my side. Even as the angry, vengeful thoughts boiled through me, I saw the sin of them. Jesus Christ had died for this man; was I going to ask for more? Lord Jesus, I prayed, forgive me and help me to forgive him."

For a long, tormenting moment Corrie wrestled with the most difficult thing she ever had to do. She knew she had to forgive because of Jesus' command: "If you do not forgive men their sins, neither will my Father in heaven forgive your sin." Still coldness clutched her heart. In desperation, she breathed a silent prayer again, "Jesus, help me! I cannot forgive him. Give me *your* forgiveness."

Corrie felt nothing, "not the slightest spark of warmth or charity," but she did manage to reach our her hand in sheer obedience. "As I did," she remembers, "an incredible thing happened. The current started in my shoulder, raced down my arm, sprang into our joined hands. And then this healing warmth seemed to flood my whole being, bringing tears to my eyes . . . I had never known God's love so intensely as I did then."

And so this courageous woman did the unthinkable: she remained open and vulnerable in the face of pain. "It is not on our forgiveness any more than on our goodness that the world's healing hinges," Corrie ten Boom discovered, "but on His. When He tells us to love our enemies, He gives, along with the command, the love itself."[3]

What is forgiveness? A gift of infinite grace.

WHY SHOULD WE FORGIVE?

The obvious reason to forgive is that God tells us to. To illustrate how important this is, Jesus told the parable of the unmerciful servant (Matthew 18:23–35). A servant who owes the king two million dollars pleads for mercy lest he be sold into slavery to pay his debt. Moved with compassion, the king cancels the entire debt. Immediately the servant goes out and grabs a man who owes him twenty dollars and demands repayment. When the king finds out about this, he is outraged and throws the unmerciful servant into jail. We will be treated in the same way, Jesus says, if we refuse to forgive others as God has forgiven us.

We forgive because we have been forgiven. Forgiveness is given to us freely, from the hand of a compassionate and gracious God, and out of the overflow of that love, we are to forgive others.

And yet even in the light of God's immense mercy, we often find it difficult—sometimes impossible—to be merciful to others. Certainly some sins seem unforgivable. Abuse. Abandonment by a parent or spouse. Betrayal. Exploitation. Physical injury. "Forgiveness is costly," says David Augsburger, "outrageously costly."[4] But unforgiveness is costly too.

THE HIDDEN COSTS OF UNFORGIVENESS

If you recall Jim Glennon's comment at the beginning of this chapter, he said that nothing contributes more to sickness than resentment. Have you ever thought you have forgiven someone, but secretly still harbored resentment? What did it do to your emotional health? Your peace of mind? *Re-sentire* means to "feel again and again." Resentment wreaks havoc with our emotions. By hugging our hurts, recalling a painful memory over and over again, we torture ourselves and can actually make ourselves emotionally sick. Nursing negative feelings can lead to depression, self-hatred, even dark leanings toward suicide.

Unforgiveness can also make us physically sick. "Resentment, bitterness, and hate all hurt and often disable those in whom they take root," observes Ken Blue. "I recently prayed over a woman with a bleeding ulcer, who was not healed until she forgave her father for sexually abusing her. Another man was healed of arthritis only after he forgave his boss for betraying him . . . Learning to forgive others is often the key which unlocks the door leading to restoration and health."[5]

We all know people whose sour countenances reflect a heart of bitterness, others whose backs actually bend under the weight of an invisible burden of resentment. To become aware of unforgiveness in your own life, ask yourself, "Where does my body store stress?" If a physical problem reoccurs frequently, you might ask, "Could my physical ailment be connected to an un-acknowleged emotional problem?" Many times unforgiveness is an unseen factor.

Unforgiveness affects every aspect of who we are. Its spiritual effects are probably the hardest to recognize and perhaps the most costly. "If you do not forgive men their sins," warns Jesus, "your heavenly Father will not forgive your sins" (Matthew 6:15 NIV). And we are told that if we cherish sin in our hearts, e.g., unforgiveness, God does not listen to our prayers (Psalm 66:18). Unforgiveness cuts off the free-flow of communcation between ourselves and the heavenly Father, whose very nature is Love.

Have you ever felt cut off from God? Could unforgiveness be a reason?

FORGIVING FROM THE HEART

In order for forgiveness to do the deep and lasting work the Spirit intends, Jesus says it must come "from the heart" (Matthew 18:35). What does this mean?

As children, we are taught to say we're sorry, to shake hands and be friends. It is a nicety, an obligation. My children tend to mumble their apologies quickly, sometimes looking at the ceiling instead of directly at the person they've hurt. I often make them write down their feelings to at least be more intentional about forgiving. Once my eight-year-old wrote: "Dear God, I'm sorry about this morning. Please help me to get my fun stuff back."

I smiled when I read that prayer. I wanted to cry too. Because that is so often how I approach forgiveness. It is something that I sail through, put a bright face on—"sorry about that!"—almost a ritual I perform in order to "get my fun stuff back"—feeling okay about myself and having others think I'm okay.

Who among us wants to face the true issues of forgiveness: taking responsibility for the hurt we've inflicted, confessing our own thoughtlessness or malice, and humbling ourselves to make things right—or conversely if we've been wounded, confronting the depth of our pain, working through it and seeing the offender as needy too.

And so we mumble our apologies when we hurt others, or keep smiling when someone hurts us, pretending it's "no big deal." By stopping short of true forgiveness, we miss true healing and the experience of knowing God's love more intensely than perhaps we ever have before, as Corrie ten Boom did.

HOW CAN WE TRULY FORGIVE?

Forgiveness is a process. It is one thing to forgive an offensive remark by a friend; it is quite another to forgive years of childhood abuse. With deep, long-standing hurts, the process usually takes longer, but regardless of how long it takes, we should celebrate every step along the way. Healing is good work and once we allow God to begin the process, He promises to complete it (Philippians 1:6). He won't stop short, and neither should we.

No matter how big or small the hurt is, I find these steps are helpful in working through the forgiveness process:

1. Identify the offender and the hurt.
2. Name the pain: note down specific feelings and reactions. How did it hurt you and what were your sinful responses?
3. Bring your hurt into the presence of Jesus, expressing all that you experienced and felt.
4. Ask Him to forgive your sinful responses.
5. Ask Him to heal your hurt.
6. Forgive the offender for each offense.
7. Ask Jesus what steps you should take to bring reconciliation.

Let's take a closer look at the process.

IDENTIFY THE OFFENDER AND THE HURT

This first step is not as obvious as it seems. You may be able immediately to identify a specific event or person that hurt you. But often because we repress hurt, these things may be covered up. How can we know what and who we need to forgive? If you have a strong negative reaction toward someone or begin to avoid that person altogether, it is possible that forgiveness is needed. If you suspect that there are people and events in your past that still cause pain, take a personal inventory, dividing your life into stages—birth to five, childhood, teen years, adulthood—write down particular incidents that were painful. This will usually reveal unhealed areas in your life.

NAME THE PAIN

Once you have identified a specific hurt, the next step is to enter into a time of prayerful reflection, asking the Lord to guide you. "Lord," you might ask, "why did that hurt me so much?" Acknowledge your feelings: "I felt rejected, belittled, neglected . . ." and your sinful reactions: "I was angry, blamed him, withdrew my affection." We cannot really forgive until we look at problems and call them by their real names.

After you have identified a hurtful incident and the pain it caused, ask God to forgive you for your sinful responses, e.g., anger, resentment, bitterness and ask Him to remove the hardness of your heart as you repent before Him. Then bring your pain to Jesus. As a small child might bring a cherished, shattered toy to a loving parent for repair, bring your broken relationships in prayer to Jesus. At this point, you no longer analyze the situation. You simply hand them over into His care—and He brings healing to situations that often seem irreparable. This can be done in several ways.

BRINGING HURT INTO THE PRESENCE OF JESUS: THREE MODELS

You may want to come into Jesus' presence through interactive prayer as we have thoughout this book: imagining yourself in a Scripture scene that will facilitate forgiveness. In the previous chapter, for example, Diane was able to forgive her mother's emotional abuse when she saw her mom as a little girl sitting in Jesus' lap receiving His love as she did.

1. Resting in the lap of Jesus. To use this prayer method yourself, imagine sitting in the lap of Jesus as we did in chapter two. Rest a while there soaking up His love, then imagine someone who has hurt you as a small child too. Invite him or her to sit in Jesus' lap with you. Tell the person honestly how you feel, how you were hurt, yet feel Jesus' love for that person too. Extend forgiveness in His name. Then confess and ask forgiveness for your own actions or attitudes that may have hurt the other person. Let Jesus wrap His arms around you both and draw you close again.

2. Facing an offender. Another way to use prayer to facilitate forgiveness is to name a person who has hurt you. Say his or her name out loud:

my father
my mother
a sibling
a friend
someone at school
someone at work
myself
God

Place that person in front of you in your mind's eye as you both stand in the presence of Jesus. If the person who has hurt you has violated you, imagine a glass barrier between you and that person: you can see the person clearly, but the person can't come close. Tell the person what he/she did that hurt you the most. Express all of your feelings. Name your hurt, your anger, your shame.

Then turn to Jesus. Ask His forgiveness for any wrong attitude on your part, e.g., anger, bitterness, hatred. Let him cleanse and restore your heart. If you can't receive Jesus' healing, it may be that you can't let go fully of the pain in order to receive healing. To let Him take the pain completely, imagine yourself standing behind the cross as you face your offender and let the deepest wounding fall on Jesus, let Him receive it onto His body on the cross. "Surely he took up our infirmities and carried our sorrows . . . and by his wounds we are healed" (Isaiah 53:4–5 NIV). Then let Jesus give you His healing, His wholeness, His identity.

Out of His love and strength choose to forgive the person. "I forgive you, _____, for _____" (be specific). Are there things for which you need to ask that person for forgiveness?

Finally, ask Jesus if there is something you need to do as an expression of your new feelings toward the person. You might want to write a letter to someone in the past (an old boyfriend, a parent who has died), then tear the letter up. Or you might want to confess what happened in your heart to someone else (James 5:16).

You may need to forgive several people. For example, if you were abused, you may need to forgive the abuser, a parent or parents perhaps whom you felt should have protected you, yourself (if you blame yourself for letting it happen), even God (if you harbor bitterness toward Him). As you walk through the process, address each offender one at a time. It is especially important to go through the same process to forgive God and yourself as you do other people.

In the next chapter, I will share a story about forgiving God. Since this chapter focuses on forgiving others, I am not able to go into the complexities of self-forgiveness. But keep in mind that it is always a factor. As Jesus asks you to be merciful to others, He asks you to be merciful to yourself. It may be particularly helpful to have another person pray with you for self-forgiveness, as a friend may be more discerning of the issues that need to be prayed through.

3. Memory healing. A third way to let Jesus help you forgive is to picture yourself with Him in a painful event as it unfolds. Angie was a young woman with overprotective parents. They were suspicious of outsiders, afraid that neighbors might be a bad influence on their daughter or harm her in some way. They were so fearful that Angie was never allowed to go outside as a child or invite friends in to play with her. As an adult, Angie harbored resentment and hatred toward her parents. She knew she needed to forgive them, but she couldn't.

Of all the hurts in her childhood, it was the utter loneliness she experienced that hurt Angie the most. As we explored how Jesus could heal this through prayer, I asked Angie what she did when she felt lonely as a child. She said she crawled under the dining room table and cried. I asked her if she could invite Jesus into her loneliness there. Yes, she could do that.

In prayer, Angie pictured herself as a child hiding under the dining room table. She started to cry, remembering the pain of having no friends, of feeling like a prisoner in her own house. We invited Jesus into that scene. He wanted to come close to Angie; to do that, we saw Him get down on His hands and knees and crawl under the table. He put His arms around her, absorbing her loneliness and infusing her with His love. In that way, Angie was finally able to empty her heart of the hatred she felt toward her parents. Then Jesus spent a while talking with Angie and playing with her like the friend she always wished she'd had.

After comforting Angie, Jesus walked over to her parents and looked at them with compassion and sadness. They were sitting on the couch looking lonely too. Angie began to look at them through His eyes, not through her hurt. Her father had been harshly treated as a child and he wanted to protect his daughter from the same fate. He was actually doing a good thing in a poor way. Angie's maternal grandmother had died when Angie's mom was a small child. Angie's mom had never learned how to play little girl games, so she always seemed distant to Angie.

Jesus put his arms around each of Angie's parents to comfort them as He had comforted her. "I love them too," Jesus said. "Can't you forgive them? They didn't know how much they were hurting you."

Looking back at a hurtful past, we tend to see things from a limited perspective and feel things from only one point of view—our own. When we bring our hurt into the presence of Jesus, He shows us the truth about the *whole* situation, about our own heart and about the hearts of others involved.

As Angie saw her parents' pain for the first time, she began to forgive them not just from her head, but from her heart. I shared a verse with Angie: "Set me free from my prison, that I may praise your name" (Psalm 142:7 NIV). I explained to Angie that unforgiveness imprisons both the accuser and the accused, while forgiveness sets both parties free. As Jesus had set Angie free from the prison of her loneliness, she in turn was able to set herself and her parents free from the prison of her unforgiveness. The key to forgiveness for Angie was that memory healing.

TAKING A STEP OF RECONCILIATION

Just as hurt perpetuates brokenness, healing energizes us too—but in a new direction. It moves us toward wholeness, toward mending what has been broken, toward reconciliation.

"The gift of forgiveness will always feel incomplete if it does not bear fruit in reconciliation," observes Marjorie Thompson.[6] Forgiveness begins by recognizing that a connection, a very precious connection between two people has been severed. Reconciliation completes the process by re-establishing that connection. A handshake, a phone call, a note or gift are all gestures of reconciliation that say, "I'm sorry. Let's begin again."

You may not feel ready to take such an action. That's okay. But you can begin immediately to bless rather than curse the offender. In Luke 6:27–28, Jesus tells us to love our enemies, those who "spitefully use us." We can do this in three ways:

- by doing good to them
- blessing them
- praying for them

Begin by changing your attitude toward the person: offering a prayer of blessing, wishing them God's best and extending as much love as you can.

As forgiveness dislodges the logjam in our hearts created by sin and hurt, blessing releases a free flow of positive feelings that carry us forward toward healing and renewal. Instead of a fist clenched around a rock in hate, the same hand is outstretched, open, ready to love again. "I will give you a new heart and put a new spirit in you," God promises, "I will remove from you your heart of stone and give you a heart of flesh" (Ezekiel 36:26 NIV).

PHIL'S STORY

If a picture is worth a thousand words, then certainly a picture of the way God heals is worth a thousand words of explanation. So I want to end this chapter with a story. It will give you an idea of how forgiveness can fully unfold in a person's life over the course of time.

I have a friend named Phil—a warm, sensitive man whose openness and affability put people immediately at ease. However, twenty-five years ago Phil was a very different person. He was an angry, tormented young man who kept people at arm's distance. What produced the dramatic change in his life? The gift of forgiveness.

The change in Phil's life took place over the course of a year just after he became a Christian in college. He was twenty years old. We'll start the story there.

Like many new Christians, Phil found that salvation was a wonderful thing, but it didn't solve all of his problems. Even after his conversion experience, hurts from the past kept surfacing in his mind—most of the pain centered around the relationship with his father, whose seething anger toward him had often boiled over in verbal abuse and beatings. When these painful memories emerged, Phil's immediate reaction was to force himself not to think about them.

One day Phil found himself remembering the hurtful experiences again. When the memories came back this time, the Lord seemed to direct him *not* to push them away, but rather to walk through them step by step.

Tentatively, Phil followed God's guidance and opened himself to healing prayer. For the first time, he dared to look at one of the memories that had caused him so much pain. He remembered being beaten by his father when he was about eight years old. Even though this happened years ago, Phil felt the same emotions that had filled his heart years ago. He found himself reliving the loneliness, hurt and betrayal all over again. But there was one important difference this time—Jesus was there.

Phil remembers: "Seeing myself once again rolled up on the floor in pain, I sensed the presence of Jesus. He was there on the floor beside me, touching me and pouring out His love. I had been weeping, but I wept all the more as I sensed His sorrow at what was happening and the love He had for me as I was going through the beating."

As Phil relived this memory, he looked toward his father and sensed that the Lord wanted him to forgive his dad. He couldn't. After a while, he said honestly, "I can't forgive. I want to be able to forgive, but I can't." At that moment, Phil felt the warmth of God's love filling his heart. He found himself uttering words he never thought he could say: "Dad, I forgive you for the beating." Phil now could recall that terrible beating as a fact in his past, not as an open wound. It was a memory that had been healed.

Over the next few months, God led Phil through many similar experiences of memory healing. Then Phil received the hardest blow of his life. During a visit home from college, his mother blurted out during an argument: "Your father hates you! He has always hated you! He was repulsed by you from the day you came home from the hospital!" Phil was stunned to discover that his father had hated him *every* day of his life.

Phil went back to school, weighed down by this thought. It crushed him. In his anguish, Phil turned to God in prayer again. God gently reminded him of the time when He had walked with Phil through hurtful memories, healing him with His love and helping him to forgive. That process needed to continue.

Phil set aside a time to be alone to do that. He prayed a prayer of protection, asking that only those things which were filtered through God's love would be able to touch him during the next few hours. Then Phil asked the Holy Spirit to guide his steps in prayer.

A particularly painful experience of abuse surfaced in his mind. Recalling the memory, Phil saw his father boiling over with rage. He had ordered Phil to go to his closet and get a belt. Phil felt humiliated and scared as he handed the belt to him. Phil's dad doubled the belt and began to hit him: the buckle hurt even more than the belt as he was lashed on the legs and back. Phil stared in anger at his father, resolving not to cry and give him the satisfaction of winning. This only enraged his father more.

Finally, Phil's mother came into the room and intervened, screaming that Phil couldn't be beaten anymore. By this time, Phil was lying on the floor, crying and huddled down, trying to deflect the kicks and blows. Reliving the memory now, Phil saw his mother shouting and pulling at the arm his dad was using to hit him, when he became aware that someone else was in the room. Next to the closet door stood Jesus. "The look on His face changed my heart forever," Phil remembers. "I could see how moved He was by the abuse and the hurt. I was so touched by His love that I could sense it healing my body and inner being. I remember feeling that no one had ever cared. Now I knew that He had been there, and if I had only been able to see Him instead of my attacker I perhaps would never have carried the hurt all those years. Suddenly the look of hatred on my dad's face, the beating and kicks, the shouting seemed to fade away.

"God's love was healing me—a love that was not only extended to me, but also to my dad and mom. My heart went out to my dad. He had lost the best years of his life. Instead of filling his life with love and caring relationships, he had burdened himself with heavy work obligations, unfulfilled expectations and anger. His lack of love had left him a pauper in the most important aspects of his life."

At that moment, God gave Phil the grace to say from his heart, "Dad, I forgive you. Up to this time I have only been able to forgive you each instance, but now I forgive *you*. I forgive *you*, Dad."

Phil was in tears, released from years of bitterness and hurt. God transformed his heart and gave him a new love for his dad. Phil knew that his love was one-way, and there were times in the ensuing years when he would fall flat on his face with resentment and the old hard feelings, but things were never the same. "There was a love kindled by the love I was learning from my heavenly Father. I had a Source greater than any anger and hate that could be leveled against me."

Today Phil is a soft-spoken, compassionate father, husband, and pastor. When he speaks from the pulpit about the Father's love, congregations are visibly moved and sense an incredible atmosphere of love in the room. Phil has a particular gift for drawing hurting men and women into the healing arms of the Father, even as he was drawn into those arms years ago.

Can you imagine what Phil's life would have looked like without forgiveness? According to research that tracks the patterns of abusive families, Phil very likely would have abused his children (and perhaps his wife) as he had been abused, a pattern that might have been repeated in successive generations. But that didn't happen. Forgiveness broke the deadly cycle of abuse and began a new cycle of health and healing.

WALKING IN STRIDE WITH GOD

"When we forgive," writes Lewis Smedes, "we create a new beginning out of a past pain that never had a right to exist in the first place . . . we ride the crest of love's cosmic wave; we walk in stride with God. And we heal the hurt we never deserved."[7]

Is there a broken relationship in your life? A hurt you never deserved? Perhaps you have tried to forgive, but can't. Or you may have begun the process, but you sense you need to take another step. Walk in stride with God. Let Him take you to a higher place in your heart, to a place of looking forward, not back; to a place of moving on toward the future, rather than being imprisoned in the past.

Before you enter into the prayerful reflection on the next page, invite the Holy Spirit to be part of the process. It is His job to draw you to Christ (John 16:14) and it is Christ who teaches us how to forgive. As those who have been wounded and as offenders ourselves, let's come close to Calvary—and experience the deep, deep love of Jesus.

THE GIFT
OF FORGIVENESS

 ead and Reflect on the Gospel accounts of the crucifixion and resurrection

"The hour has come," said Jesus. "Look, the Son of Man is betrayed into the hands of sinners" . . . then all the disciples deserted him and fled . . .

So the soldiers took charge of Jesus. Carrying his own cross, he went out to the place of the skull (which in Aramaic is called Golgotha). Here they crucified him. Jesus said, "Father, forgive them, for they don't know what they are doing . . ."

Picture yourself at Calvary. Golgotha. The place of the skull, a hard, dark hill set against a stony sky. People are milling about, soldiers, onlookers. Suddenly you see Jesus, arms outstretched on a rough, wooden cross. You hear the pounding of a hammer and see His body flinch with each piercing blow.

As the nails are driven in, you shudder, horrified to see Him suffer. How can they do this? Don't they know Him? Don't they love Him as you do? You feel full of rage.

Then . . . something in you grows silent. You know that you have helped nail Him there, for who of us is so righteous that we can stand apart and say that He is dying for someone else's sins?

Take a moment to contemplate Jesus hanging on the cross. Look at His feet, feet that struggled step by step up the steep, hard climb to Calvary, feet that staggered as Jesus bent under the burden of a hundred-pound cross beam dragged on His shoulders through the streets of Jerusalem. Feet that never stopped . . . despite the pain, the agony of His excruciating journey. A journey He walked for you.

Now look at Jesus' hands. Hands that only loved, only reached out to heal; hands brutally bound, then pierced through. Outstretched. Always outstretched, embracing the world, drawing all the viciousness, all the hatred, all the pain out of human hearts so that the Father can fill them with His love.

Now look into Jesus' eyes. Let them pierce your heart. Enter into His suffering and let Him enter into yours. Wait in silence, letting His gaze of mercy go deep.

If there is hurt . . .

> that you can no longer bear, let it flow out to Jesus. Let Him bear your grief and carry your sorrows.

If there is sin . . .

> give it to Jesus through confession and let Him give you His forgiveness. *I have paid the price,* says Jesus. *My love covers a multitude of sins.*

There are others who stand at the foot of the cross with you also in need of compassion and forgiveness. You become aware of someone standing on your left side and someone else on your right. The person on the left is someone who has hurt you. The person on the right is someone you have hurt.

Take a moment to imagine who these people might be. Write their names below.

Jesus looks at your offender with the same love in His eyes that He had for you. Then He looks at you. "As I have forgiven you," says Jesus, "can you not forgive this one who has wounded you? Can you not see (_____) with My eyes, needy as you are? Release (_____) as I have released you, embrace (_____) as I have embraced you." You feel a river of mercy flowing inexplicably out of your heart toward this one whom you have kept at arm's length.

Then Jesus looks at the person on your right, the one you have wounded in some way. Jesus knows (_____)'s pain and longs to heal it, but He needs your help. "And this one you have hurt," He asks, "is there not something you can do to restore (_____) as I have restored you?" A moment ago you were so aware of your own hurt, but somehow you fail to see how much you can hurt others. A cutting word, a harsh action, perhaps a sin unseen—judgment, condemnation. "I'm so sorry, please forgive me." You reach out to draw your friend close again.

And so Calvary, the place of woundedness, becomes a place of healing. You have experienced a kind of love that is rare and costly. Life-changing. As Jesus walked the road to Calvary, He asks us to do the same. To learn to love even if it kills us. And that is, in the end, what it is supposed to do. Kill our self-centeredness, our need for self-justification and vindication. It will be difficult, sometimes it may seem impossible, but Jesus promises to be with us to empower us and to keep us faithful.

THE GIFT
OF PEACE

"I am leaving you with a gift—peace of mind and heart! And the peace I give isn't fragile like the peace the world gives. So don't be troubled or afraid."
—John 14:27 (TLB)

*A*fter I tell stories at retreats like the ones in the previous chapter, invariably someone will come up and say, "I've had a happy childhood. I didn't come from a dysfunctional family. I didn't suffer abuse or neglect, nothing traumatic. Why do I need healing?"

I can sympathize with someone who says this because I was fortunate enough to grow up in a family that provided the love and nurture I needed. I'm married now to a man who loves me and I have two happy well-adjusted children. (Needless to say, that doesn't mean there is an absence of strife in our household!)

But I've found that even for those of us who enjoy relatively secure lives, there are times when an unexpected crisis can sweep away our comfortable moorings and leave us adrift in fear. Sometimes just feeling overwhelmed by the battles of daily living can erode our sense of well-being, sucking us into a maelstrom of depression and despair. The gift of peace is one way God pours the balm of His healing love over our troubled hearts and heals anxiety and fear—the anxiety and fears we are aware of and those we're not conscious of at all.

SURPRISED BY GRACE

I first discovered how powerful the gift of God's peace could be during a family vacation one summer in northern Wisconsin. I wasn't confronting a crisis, I wasn't feeling heavy-hearted. In fact, I was feeling quite peaceful . . . I thought.

Our family had just come back from a long day of sightseeing. As soon as we returned to the woodland resort where we were staying, the girls headed off on bikes, and my husband, Larry, and my mom went to play tennis. My father and I felt a need for quiet after being cooped up in a noisy, crowded car.

We both looked at the lake. It lay quietly at dusk—vast, spread out, still. The stillness seemed to beckon us. It was as if its stillness were delicious, some new, inviting flavor we longed to taste. My father and I looked at each other at the same time and said, "Let's go for a canoe."

We put on parkas, then headed for shore and found a canoe beached on the rocks. We were in high spirits, relaxed and laughing. As Dad stepped into the back end of the canoe jauntily, one foot slipped on a rock, soaking his shoe. *Squiiish!*

I winced, inwardly sighing with disappointment that our venture had been sabotaged.

I glanced at him, anticipating a look of disgust or aggravation, feeling a vague sense of guilt that it must be *my* fault that his shoes were ruined. "Want to go back and change?" I asked.

"No." He shook his head. "Never mind."

"But aren't those your *new* shoes?" I felt distressed for him.

He nodded and smiled. "Guess I'm just gettin' old. Not as agile as I used to be. Don't worry about it."

The incident obviously didn't bother Dad. Why should it bother me? The tightness in my stomach began to ease.

We grabbed our paddles and pushed off, eager to get out on the water. Our strokes were choppy at first, since we both were out of practice paddling, but they soon smoothed out. The canoe slid quietly through the water, sending silent ripples across the surface of the lake. As the sun set, the world was awash with color, blurred softly like an Impressionistic painting. The reflections of trees, blue-green, turning amber in the evening light, undulated along the edges of the shore. The sky was bathed in gold, then pink, then a rosy hue.

Entering into that deep peace was like easing slowly into a soothing tub of hot water. My muscles relaxed, my mind stilled to a whisper.

Dad and I didn't say anything as we dug our paddles deep into the water. I think we both felt that the silence was sacred. We seemed swallowed up by it. The broad, sweeping panorama of water and sky all around us filled us with awe. Our spirits seemed to expand. It was more than a sense of stillness and peace that I felt at that moment; it was a sense of holiness and wholeness. I felt keenly aware of God's presence. The supernatural seemed to permeate everything natural: the flash of a fish breaking through the quiet surface of the lake, a flock of gulls that winged upward and silently stole away as we paddled close. The world at that moment seemed completely at rest.

I wanted to linger there forever, just soaking up the stillness. We stopped our paddling at times and let the canoe drift, our paddles across our knees, smiling at each other. There was no need to speak. I felt a quiet intimacy with my father, as we both experienced something too deep to understand, too wonderful to express in words.

Soon, too soon, the sky grew dark and we reluctantly agreed to head home. The canoe beached, we walked back to join the family, the silence of the lake at our backs. And that was it. Just one memory of many in a family vacation.

But that wasn't *it* for me. For months afterwards, long after Mom and Dad had flown home and I was caught up in a thousand other things, I would sit at my dining room table and have my devotions. As I opened my heart in prayer, the experience my Dad and I shared on the lake that summer kept coming back. It would float to the surface of my mind while I was praying about something else. I didn't know why. It was an enjoyable memory and I felt that sense of deep peace when I recalled it, but I began to wonder if there was something more in that experience that I hadn't gleaned.

"Lord, what are you trying to teach me?" I began to ask.

And slowly, as I let the Holy Spirit, who knows the "deep things of God," reveal what it was, I came to see the gift I'd been given. My dad and I had not only experienced a holy moment of tranquility in nature, but something about that moment also brought a sense of inner wholeness between us. It began to dawn on me that, after that moment, I thought of my dad in a new way. Something fractured in our relationship had been put right.

As I said earlier, I've never had major conflicts with my dad. And so I wondered, what could there possibly be in my relationship with my Dad that even needed healing?

Looking back on that day, I remembered that one jarring moment when Dad soaked his shoe as he slipped getting into the canoe. My immediate reaction was one of anxiety, guilt, defensiveness, false responsibility, a whole host of unhealthy feelings that can build up between two people enmeshed in one another's lives over years. Why did I overreact to such a minor aggravation?

Part of my overreaction was probably due to the fact that I resented our "perfect day" being ruined by something that went wrong. Who was to blame? My dad? Me? Of course, no one was to blame; it was simply an accident. Part of my overreaction may have been due to a compulsive need to control people and situations. My dad is intrinsically this way too, but he was learning to let go of his perfectionistic tendencies and laugh at his mistakes.

So many of our relationships with loved ones are fraught with unspoken tensions like these: blaming and shaming, an unhealthy need to be in control, exacting unfair expectations and demands on others, on ourselves. These are subtle things, the kind of everyday things that put undue stress on our relationships, the kinds of things most of us ignore or never acknowledge.

Unhealthy patterns such as these can only be cured by "experiencing God's unconditional grace at the deepest level of our beings."[1] That's the kind of healing I experienced that day when I was first infused with God's peace. Like C. S. Lewis who was "surprised by joy," as he first recognized a supernatural beauty and goodness beyond the natural world, I was "surprised by grace." God's presence was so pervasive in that experience, that inexplicably, in a moment of grace, much of the hidden tension between my dad and me was washed away as the sun had washed the lake with a golden glow that evening.

After that experience, I felt a new acceptance toward my

father. I felt more relaxed, more free to be myself and to let him be himself. The new freedom in our relationship also made me more aware of the unfair demands and expectations I place on people I am close to. In my family, in my friendships, I began to consciously cultivate an atmosphere of grace.

The hidden tensions that I've been talking about may seem like little things. Certainly they do not ravish lives like the devastating pain of abuse and abandonment, but they do cause hurt. And I have come to see that God is every bit as concerned about the "little things"—the unacknowledged destructive patterns of behavior that sabotage the joy in our relationships—as He is with the more obvious heart hurts that cry out for healing.

THE INVISIBLE DISEASE

When Jesus promises to provide peace of mind and heart, I believe His promise applies to anything in our lives that causes "dis-ease." As doctors warn us, undercurrents of stress and tension that run beneath the surface of our relationships with other people and within ourselves can cause physical problems: headaches, ulcers, high blood pressure, muscle tension, depression, and even cancer. Stress is a kind of "invisible disease" that we need to take seriously.

"The thief does not come except to steal, and to kill, and to destroy," said Jesus. "I have come that they may have life, and that they may have it more abundantly" (John 10:10). I'm convinced that one of the ways Satan "steals" our inner peace and seeks to destroy our well-being is by stress and tension that build up unseen when we fail to resolve conflicts, overtax our minds and bodies, or ignore sin. If you are not enjoying life to the full as Jesus intended, He will do everything He can to help you recognize and deal with unhealthy tendencies—however small—that harm you.

What is the antidote to stress?

SHALOM: PEACE WITHIN OURSELVES

"Some years ago I found myself, when praying for sick people, increasingly using the word 'peace,'" writes Michael Harper. "I would actually speak 'peace' to diseased tissue and infections. I nearly always used the Hebrew word *shalom*. More recently I have discovered that this is the closest word in the Old Testament for 'health.' It means more than the absence of war, stress, and tension. It declares a state of wholeness . . . They (the Hebrews) believed that *shalom* was the best word to describe a man in a state of wholeness, of being what the Creator had always intended."[2]

God is not only concerned with our healing, but also with our health, our general state of well-being. He really wants us to be as whole and happy as He originally intended—to enjoy our relationships with others, with Him, with ourselves.

When I described my relationship with my dad earlier in this chapter, I said that we got along very well. Yet I discovered that there were hidden areas of tension between us that still caused "dis-ease." God "spoke peace" to these troubled areas and brought a new sense of wholeness to our relationship that surprised me.

In the same way, He can speak a word of peace to undo stress in our own hearts. Years ago I went to a healing conference held by Francis MacNutt. There were times when Father MacNutt prayed for the whole auditorium of people, asking us to participate in different ways. At one point (I cannot even remember what he was praying for specifically), he asked the audience to stand up as he prayed. With my eyes closed in prayer, I held out my hands, palms up, a gesture of receptivity toward what the Lord would do. Suddenly I felt a strange sensation in my hands, as if long strands of spaghetti were being drawn out of the ends of my fingertips. The sensation was so real I opened my eyes and looked down at my hands to see what was happening. Of course, I saw nothing.

But I felt dramatically different. An incredible sense of deep rest came over me. A profound peace. It was as if every muscle in my body, every tissue, every cell was completely relaxed.

I realized that those long tendrils of tension that had been drawn out of my body were in some way tangible manifestations of stress that had literally tied up my insides in knots. (Several years earlier, I had been diagnosed with intermittent bowel syndrome, a condition that made my intestines contract, causing severe abdominal pain. I suffered these intestinal attacks particularly during times of stress.)

I *had* been under a lot of stress that week, taking carloads of friends from church to the conference to train them for a healing meeting we were going to conduct soon. It had been a very intense time, and carrying the responsibility for the upcoming event added even more stress. Stress, I told myself, was just part of being a leader. But what gratitude and relief I felt when I experienced that deep rest. How I needed it! I assumed that stress was just a necessary evil one had to live with, but maybe God didn't think so.

At the end of the service, Francis MacNutt asked anyone who had received healing to raise their hand. I wanted to raise mine. But what would people think? Stress was such a minor thing. I hadn't thrown away crutches or been cured of arthritis or felt released from demonic oppression. And yet I did feel released and healed in some way.

After that evening's session, we followed the crowd to the parking lot. My car was blocked in and we had to make our way slowly, very slowly, through a massive traffic jam. Usually in that situation, I feel anxious, frustrated, often angry and impatient. But the feeling of deep rest I had experienced earlier continued, even in that stressful situation. I was amazed.

As I drove home after letting off my passengers, I reached to turn on the radio. I was accustomed to turning on soft, soothing music for relaxation. But I sensed that even that "peaceful" music would be too loud and jarring, disturbing the deep peace I cherished with wonder within me. I wanted that incredible feeling to last as long as possible. And it did last for several days.

Being infused with the gift of God's peace revealed to me what a stress-free body could feel like. It was fabulous! The experience was so wonderful that I wanted it to be more than a brief and fleeting "feeling." I wanted it to be a permanent part of who I was. I began to change my lifestyle so that deep peace which I had tasted briefly could be incorporated more consciously into the abundant life Jesus wanted me to live.

In order to do this, I had to take a good, hard look at the way I was living. I had been under pressure during the time of the healing conference, but much of that stress had been self-induced: feeling overly responsible for other people, overly anxious about preparations for the event I was planning, overly worried about its success being bound up with my own self-image. I had allowed some unhealthy patterns to get a stranglehold on my life.

To restore my wholeness, my *shalom*, I had to learn to untie these knots that caused emotional stress, and I had to learn to take better care of myself physically. I developed new habits. You might find these "stress-stoppers" helpful too:

- exercise regularly to release internalized stress
- take time to relax and play
- cut down on overcommitments
- be more honest and open in interpersonal relationships
- have unhurried quiet times that allow the Holy Spirit to bathe you in His peace

SHALOM: PEACE WITH OTHERS

Hidden anxieties not only trouble our own hearts, but they also effect other people who care about us. Our society does not handle stress well. In our highly individualistic culture, we are taught to keep tension inside, to put a brave face on problems, not daring to admit to ourselves or anyone else that we can't handle them on our own. Ironically, when we need help the most from those we love, we find ourselves pushing them away.

The Bible paints a very different picture of how we should relate to one another. "We are members of one another" . . . "Bear one another's burdens, and so fulfill the law of Christ" (Ephesians 4:25; Galatians 6:2). The Body of Christ is a closely-woven community where we are intended to share our sorrows and joys, to shoulder each other's burdens, and receive and give help when needed. No man or woman should ever be an island in the sea of God's love.

Stan learned this the hard way. Stan, a popular businessman in our community, ran a successful company, had a spacious home and loving family. He never appeared to have a worry in the world. But at one point, his life began to spin out of control: his business began to fail; loss of income and credit calls caused stress at home. Disagreements with his wife turned into war. He and Sue became more and more isolated from one another, living in separate rooms, conducting separate lives. Even though Stan was leading a quiet life of desperation, he kept smiling.

However, close Christian friends began to sense that something was wrong. "You're depressed, aren't you," said a friend one day at lunch.

"What are you talking about?" Stan was offended at his friend's audacity and tried to ignore the comment.

Stan's friend was persistent. He had dealt with depression himself and knew the signs. He said he could see it in Stan's telltale face and in his attitude as he tried to be pragmatic and unemotional to mask his lack of control—almost to a point of harshness. Stan left the restaurant in a huff.

The next day when Stan walked into his office, he checked his voice mail to find another message from a Christian friend. The friend said he had been praying for Stan and sensed that Stan was facing difficulties. He reminded Stan that God loved him and assured him that everything would be okay. He just had to hang in there. Stan leaned back in his chair and gazed out the window of his tenth-story office, listening to the message over and over again.

That afternoon, Stan walked into a small meeting of parents who were organizing a Young Life chapter at the local high school. Several of Stan's close friends were there. I was at the meeting, but only knew Stan as an acquaintance. Stan strolled in in his usual jovial manner, but he looked fatigued.

We began to pray for our endeavor. In the presence of the Holy Spirit, we soon shed our professional roles—as business people, teachers, homemakers—and became needy men and women before the Lord. The objective of the meeting was not at all to pray for one another, but tenderly the Holy Spirit led that way.

As Stan prayed, I seemed to see Jesus walk across the room and put His hand on Stan's shoulder. A picture flashed across my mind of Stan as Atlas, trying to carry the weight of the world on his shoulders. Stan was straining and groaning under an immense burden. Jesus seemed to reveal to me in that moment that He wanted that burden to roll off Stan's back.

I felt the Holy Spirit nudging me to get up from my chair and put my hands on Stan's shoulders. I was dumbfounded. How could I do that? I hardly knew the people there. This wasn't a prayer meeting; we were praying for the high school.

I still felt the nudging. It wouldn't go away. This felt like one of those uncomfortable moments when I had to step out in faith, not having any idea of the outcome. Hesitantly, I decided to follow through on the guidance I'd been given.

I waited for the group to pause in prayer. "Stan," I said, getting up from my chair, "this may sound strange, but I feel the Lord wants me to lay hands on you." Stan had never experienced the "laying on of hands," but he didn't object.

I walked across the room and stood behind Stan's chair, putting my hands on his shoulders. Stan's friends gathered around him and put a hand gently on him to express their love. As soon as we did this, Stan broke down in deep, uncontrollable sobs. It was as if some massive dam that had been holding back all of his emotions had suddenly burst open. His whole body shook as he released the tension that had built up inside him.

One by one, Stan's friends offered heartfelt prayers: words of healing, comfort and encouragement. God gave me a verse of Scripture for Stan: "Cast all your anxiety on him because he cares for you" (1 Peter 5:7 NIV). It was as if Jesus Himself were offering this personal invitation: *cast all your anxiety on me, Stan, because I care for you.*

Stan knew as he had never known before how much Jesus cared for him. Our hands, our words were a tangible embodiment of that concern. We literally were the Body of Christ to Stan at that moment.

As we prayed, I saw that invisible burden on Stan's back literally roll off. In my mind's eye, I now saw Stan as a little boy, as perhaps three or four years old, being carried on his Father's shoulders. He was grinning from ear to ear, carefree, and jubilant. What a reversal! The prayer picture began with Stan carrying a weight he could not bear and it ended with him carrying no weight at all and, actually, the one *being* carried. Stan left the meeting that day a different man than when he first arrived. He had come in looking fatigued and drained, and left effusive and energetic. "Forget the office!" he announced with a big grin on his face. "I'm going home and cut the grass!"

❦

Stan told me later how incredible that experience had been. He had left the house that morning "mad as hell," angry at everything: his wife, his life, his prospects, his responsibilities. After our lunchtime meeting, he called his wife to apologize and ask her forgiveness. He wrote in his journal that day:

"Feeling emancipated beyond description, and free of such oppressive burden, I started mowing the lawn at 3:00 that afternoon, had no interest in the office or anything else for that matter. For the next hour and a half, I sang at the top of my lungs."

The peace that was poured out on Stan during our prayer time was so powerful that even his wife, who wasn't there, felt the impact. "As soon as I came home that afternoon and walked into our house," she recalls, "I felt a sense of deep peace. The tension was gone. Completely gone. Stan had said on the phone, 'I love you, Sue. Everything is going to be all right.' I knew then that everything *was* going to be all right."

God's peace, a peace that passes understanding, had restored Stan's marriage. Weeks later he wrote me a note: "Sue and I are enjoying a new and wonderful relationship, focusing on each other as if we were nineteen again. Our economic problem is still there, but we keep it all in stride, and know that too shall pass. That's life!"

SHALOM: AT PEACE WITH GOD

When we are at war within ourselves, we eventually become aware of it—our bodies tell us. When our relationships break down with other people, we know that too. But what about our relationship with God? What if that breaks down? So far we've talked about physical distress and emotional distress. Now let's turn our attention to spiritual distress. How does that rob us of peace?

Most of us are familiar with the miracle in the Gospels where Jesus calms the storm on the Sea of Galilee. A sudden, violent squall comes up while the disciples are sailing across to Gerasenes. Terrified at the mounting waves that threaten to swamp the boat, the disciples call for Jesus' help. Jesus wakes up from a deep sleep, calmly comes up on deck, stretches out His hand and commands the wind and waves to be still. Immediately the wind dies down and the sea is completely calm.

What happens after that incident is just as important, but is often overlooked. As soon as Jesus gets to the other side of the lake, He is met by a man with an evil spirit. With the same authority that He uses to calm the storm that everyone can see,

Jesus speaks a word of command to the unseen storm that is raging within this man. Once the man is set free from the evil that torments him, he is subdued, Scripture says, and returns to his "right mind." He is at peace within himself.

Spiritual distress is like an inner storm. It can cause turbulence and confusion and make a person miserable. I once prayed for a woman who was tormented in this way.

Allison came to a healing conference because she knew she needed God's love. However, she didn't want to come close to God. She resisted with everything in her. A couple of friends asked me to pray for Allison because they were concerned about her. Should she leave the conference, they wondered? Every time an invitation was given for participants to draw close to God in prayer, Allison's stomach seized up, causing her terrible pain.

Allison grew tense when I came near her. Guarded and afraid, she didn't want anyone to come close to her. To put her at ease, I suggested we try a simple prayer picturing her as a little child sitting in Jesus' lap. Most people find this comfortable and relaxing. "No," Allison stiffened. "I don't want to do that."

As we were discussing this, one of Allison's friends imagined Allison as a little girl peeking around a door, wanting to come out, but timidly holding back. This was a perfect picture of Allsion's ambivalence: there was a tug-of-war going on inside her as she felt drawn toward Jesus, yet repelled at the same time.

I spent an hour and a half talking to Allison and listening to her, trying to win her trust.

Then I told her that I knew what was causing her stomach pains and if she wanted to stay at the conference, we needed to deal with it in prayer. It is not unusual when a person begins to move toward healing that a strongly opposing force works to keep the person away from getting help. I felt in this case that a demonic spirit was causing Allison's inner turbulence, especially since it became particularly intense during prayer.

I felt a spirit of rejection was causing her stomach to seize up. We needed to take authority over it and command it to leave in Jesus' name (see chapter five). I told her I could pray silently if that made her more comfortable. No, she said, she wanted to hear what I said.

So that's what we did. Stroking Allison's shoulder gently to reassure her, I prayed for the Lord's peace to flow into her. As I touched her, I sensed that the Holy Spirit was washing over her with waves of warmth. Then softly, but firmly, I used Jesus' authority to command the spirit of rejection to leave and asked the Lord to fill her with His love. Instantly, her whole body relaxed and went limp, the stiffness gone. Allison smiled, relieved.

The next day I prayed with Allison again. She was no longer tense, but she still looked sad and distraught. The session was on forgiveness and participants were encouraged to name their hurts and give their pain to Jesus so they could forgive whoever had hurt them. Allison named a long litany of hurts in her past. I put out my hands in prayer and asked her to imagine my hands as Jesus' hands. I had her trace her fingertips over the palms of my hands, imagining Jesus' wounds, even feeling the deep nail prints in the center of His hands. "See, I have engraved you on the palms of my hands" (Isaiah 49:16 NIV). Her pain was etched deeply into His hands.

Putting her hands on mine, I asked her to tell God honestly how she felt; to give Him her anger, her rage, to express her true feelings. At first she couldn't do this. She trembled with great emotion but still held back. We prayed for the freedom for her to release what was in her heart. Then she let loose. A torrent of angry feelings came pouring out with tears.

"Why did Jesus have to suffer? Why did I have to suffer? Why was I raped not once, but twice? Why does my mother hate me? Why did my boyfriend leave me? Why do I get migraines? It isn't fair. It isn't fair."

Allison had never allowed herself to express her feelings of outrage to God. But how viable is a relationship if you can't express your true heart? Allison needed to know that she could tell God anything, even her negative feelings, and yes, even forgive Him, and in turn let Him forgive her.

Aside from letting go of her anger toward God, Allison had kept her own pain bottled up inside and taken in the pain and darkness of others who had hurt her. She needed to confess these things and let them go too. After she did this, I pronounced forgiveness in Jesus' name.

I then asked Allison to turn her hands so that her palms were facing up to receive the gifts of God. This was a critical moment, Allison told me later. "I knew that I would have to give up my burdens completely to Jesus—something I had resisted because I didn't want Him to experience some of the things I had. For an instant, I considered saying no. And then it suddenly became clear to me that Jesus died on the cross for this very reason. *He died for me!* I turned my hands up and literally felt twenty pounds of darkness being lifted off my being. And in its place, I felt God's love pouring into me and restoring me."

Allison was joyous after our prayer ended. "I feel light as a feather," she said incredulously.

A couple of days later, Allison came up and threw her arms around me to thank me. She looked radiant and buoyant. "You'll never believe this," she exclaimed, "but I actually laughed five hours straight yesterday. *Five* hours!" She added, "And you know that little girl hiding behind the door? I saw her fling open the door and fly into Jesus' arms." As Allison said this, she threw open her arms in complete abandon and beamed.

What a tranformation! Allison's sad, wounded eyes now sparkled. She was free, wonderfully free to embrace God, other people, herself. Certainly she hadn't worked through all her pain, but what a breakthrough. The storm within her had subsided, lifted. Finally, she could rest peacefully within the loving arms of Someone who could carry her through whatever she faced in the future.

PEACE, BE STILL!

We all go through storms in life. Whether we are caught up in the agitation of little daily traumas that tear away at our peace of mind, or face real fears that rage within our hearts, Jesus can calm any storm with a word: "Peace, be still!" When the disciples first witnessed Jesus' power to bring peace, they were amazed: "Who can this be, that even the wind and sea obey Him!" (Mark 4:41). We will be amazed too.

The gift of peace can come quietly, unexpectedly—as you gaze at the soft glow of a candle during a hushed quiet time, as you walk in the woods and feel God close. It can come even in a glimpse out the window, as your eye beholds the beauty outside. It can come through the loving gesture of a friend. It can come through laughter or tears . . . or simply silence. It can come through prayer.

"Peace be to you," said Jesus. To *you*. In prayer, now, let Jesus speak a special word of peace to you.

THE GIFT
OF PEACE

 ead and Reflect
on Mark 4:35–39

On the same day, when evening had come, He said to them, "Let us cross over to the other side." Now when they left the multitude, they took Him along in the boat as He was . . . And a great windstorm arose, and the waves beat into the boat, so that it was already filling. But He was in the stern, asleep on a pillow. And they awoke Him and said to Him, "Teacher, do You not care that we are perishing?" Then He arose and rebuked the wind, and said to the sea, "Peace, be still!" And the wind ceased and there was a great calm.

Picture yourself gripped with fear on a stormy sea. The deck underneath you is shifting, rolling, as waves rise and swell. All around you the tempest swirls. Wave after wave dumps a deluge of water on deck, making the boat sink deeper into the sea. The wind whips at your face. "Steady, steady," you whisper. To yourself? To the wind?

You feel so helpless. "Don't you care, Lord? Don't your care?" you cry out in terror.

Seconds go by. Minutes? Hours? You are suspended in chaos, feeling lost, overwhelmed by a situation that is totally out of your control . . .

Suddenly you feel a hand on your shoulder, firm, comforting. You look around.

It's Jesus. You remember as a child tossing and turning at night in the grips of a bad dream . . . suddenly someone would be there, your mom or dad, to rescue you from imagined terrors that rocked your world. Their love, like a healing balm, brought stillness, quietness, centeredness.

That's how you feel now. The presence of Jesus is soothing. His touch radiates peace, stilling the turmoil in your soul. Even in the center of the storm, you feel an inexplicable calm.

Jesus turns then to the wind and waves that rage out of control, taking authority over them. "Peace, be still!" He stretches out His hands, subduing the storm, restoring order to the universe. He commands stillness, and the wind subsides to a whisper. The sea settles into a deep calm. You're filled with awe.

The stillness comes almost as a secret, a soft flooding of the Spirit that imparts rest to the world, to you. You look at your hands and smile. What could they command? And yet so many times you try to manage situations that are clearly out of your control, turning to prayer only as a last resort.

You look at the sea now, tamed by the touch of Jesus. How much more settled your life could be if you laid your heart open more often to receive that touch of peace. A new prayer emerges in your heart: *Come near, Lord, come near—not just in crisis, but while I'm waking, while I'm sleeping—and infuse my every action, every word, every thought with Your peace.*

THE GIFT
OF REFRESHMENT

*"Whoever drinks of the water that I shall give him will
never thirst. But the water that I shall give him will
become in him a fountain of water springing up into
everlasting life."*

—*John 4:14*

"Mid-forties . . . hmmm . . . many losses begin to occur:
cars and furniture and towels are all wearing out,"
writes a friend. "Our bodies ache. Our children win more and
more of the competitions. One by one they're leaving home;
Chris heads off to college next fall. And we know more and
more just how little we do know."

Can you sense the weariness in these words? It is a weariness
we all share as we punch in, day in and day out, on the time-
clocks of our lives: raising children, commuting to work, struggling to pay bills, serving on committees, running marathons.
In the midst of midlife, in the midst of midday, how we need

the gift of refreshment, a new infusion of energy to revive our zest for living!

Life is tiring, demanding, often draining. No one knows our tiredness, our emptiness better than Jesus. And so He calls us to be filled up with His love: "Come! Whoever is thirsty, let him come take the free gift of the water of life" (Revelation 22:17 NIV). He promises to water the dry places of our lives and satisfy our deepest thirsts with living water that springs up, cool and vibrant, providing an ever-renewable source of refreshment.

How can the gift of refreshment bring us real and lasting fulfillment and be a perpetual spring that renews us day by day? How does God use refreshment to bring healing? This is what we're going to explore now.

AN INVITATION

Do you remember the Gospel story of the woman at the well? This is where Jesus first makes His offer of "living water." The scene is a desert village, Sychar, in Samaria.

A tired, lonely woman, carrying a heavy water jar on her shoulder in the heat of the day, comes to draw water at a well. Jesus is sitting at the well, resting from a journey. The woman is disappointed to see someone sitting there. She comes to the well intentionally at noon to avoid the stares and whispers of others who know her reputation. The last thing the woman wants is to confront a stranger.

And yet something unexpected happens. As the woman draws close to the well, her eyes meet the stranger's. They are welcoming, kind. Jesus asks her for a drink of water. She is taken aback. A Jew asking a Samaritan for a drink? A man talking to a woman?

Much to her surprise, Jesus engages her in conversation. Slowly He wins her trust and she begins to feel at ease. He looks at her with compassion and understanding, as if she is someone He wants to know. Someone of value. Drinking in that look of love touches and refreshes the barrenness in her heart and satisfies a deep thirst that she didn't even know she had.

He seems to know about her inner thirst. The water that you draw at the well, He says, doesn't last. It doesn't really satisfy, but I can give you "living water" that will bubble up within you like a perpetual spring quenching your thirst always.

It is a mysterious phrase, "living water." She doesn't understand it, but something in her longs for what this Man speaks of and something in her knows that He can give it to her.

"Where can I get this water?" the woman asks.

"It's a free gift," Jesus answers. "Give me the empty cup of your heart and I will fill it to overflowing."

This is also an invitation Jesus extends to each of us. *Give me the empty cup of your heart and I will fill it to overflowing,* He says. How can we receive the gift of living water Jesus has to offer? In order to drink deeply of His love, our hearts first have to be open and receptive, ready to receive what He wants to give.

EMPTYING YOUR CUP

When I told the story of the woman at the well at a retreat one time, there was a glistening, spring-fed lake just outside the window of the retreat center where I was speaking. I held up a porcelain cup. "Imagine this as the cup of your heart," I said to the women there. "Now think of the lake outside. The immensity of God's love for each of us is hard to imagine. Proportionally, it's like that huge, vast amount of water being poured into this tiny cup."

As I said in an earlier chapter, we are pure capacity for God.[1] What a wonderful thought, but, sadly, we limit our capacity by filling our hearts with other things. Instead of experiencing an overflow of God's love, we settle for a trickle.

The cups of our hearts *are* full, but not with God. I shared with my friends at the retreat some of the things that fill the cup of my heart. I held up a set of keys—a car key, a house key—symbolizing material possessions that require a lot of my time and energy. A clipboard with a long "to-do" list represented endless responsibilities, a telephone represented relationships, a mirror suggested occupation (obsession?) with self, a handkerchief worry, binoculars represented the time I spend looking for "fears on the horizon" that never materialize, photos of loved ones spoke of other people's expectations. The list could go on and on.

Some of these are good things, eg. material possessions are useful if they don't "use" us; some of our responsibilities include serving others, which is important; and certainly we need to nurture our relationships. But any of these "good things" can become major preoccupations that crowd out space in our hearts that God wants to fill.

How can we empty our hearts to create space for God? We do it with care and deliberate intention. Just as Mary made a conscious decision to sit quietly at the feet of Jesus while her task-oriented sister Martha was caught up in the flurry of doing many things, so we need to turn *away* from our compulsive busyness and turn *toward* Jesus. Jesus is not in a hurry: He has all the time in the world. He is Lord over time. As we synchronize the frantic racing of our own internal clocks with the quiet, steady rhythms of His heart, we being to slow down and let go . . .

Just as the woman at the well put her heavy jar down, her

responsibilities, her worries, we lay aside our preoccupations. We rest, relax, wait, and listen. The wider we open our hearts, the more fully the Spirit of God can enter in.

I often find that just setting aside time to focus on God does not necessarily mean my heart is completely open to Him. I have to create psychological as well as physical space to welcome His presence. To increase my inner receptivity to the Spirit, I sometimes gaze at a candle to still the whirlwind of my thoughts, or I contemplate something of natural beauty, perhaps a lilac bud in springtime that evokes awe and wonder. Sometimes I let music wash over me and draw me into worship. I use my body to worship, sometimes lifting my hands, at other times bowing before the Lord, or dancing. Sometimes I enter into a deep silence.

Something *refreshing* is "pleasantly new and different, unusual." Are your devotional times pleasantly new and different? These special times can become so routine and stale that our hearts are closed even if we have set aside time to focus on God. I find that the more creative and fresh I keep these times, the more they refresh me.

Developing an inner receptivity to the Spirit should be something we strive for moment by moment, not just day by day. One morning I was standing at a bus stop. The hot July day before had been oppressive and stifling. That morning I was thankful for a brisk invigorating breeze: it tasted like spearmint gum and felt cool as a mountain stream. One of the words for Holy Spirit in the Bible is *pneuma*, wind. I watched the wind buffeting the high tree tops. It seemed that everywhere God was whispering, "I'm here. I'm here." I opened my heart wide to receive His gift of refreshment.

"You send forth Your Spirit . . . and You renew the face of the earth," said the Psalmist (Psalm 105:30). That summer morning, God renewed the face of the earth . . . and me.

THE GIFT OF REFRESHMENT: REST

We can experience God's refreshment in different ways. For example, when I stood at that bus stop on that hot July morning and received the gift of refreshment, I experienced that moment in three distinct ways. Even though I stood on a busy street watching a steady stream of cars whiz by, I felt *rested*—somehow taken away from that dizzying pace, and allowed to feel calm instead of frantic inside. Despite the gasoline smells and dirt of the city, I felt *purified* by the freshness of the Holy Spirit, and instead of feeling weighted down by the chores I had to do, I felt a sudden surge of *joy.* Rest, purity, joy are all aspects of refreshment. Let's look at examples of each.

Going back to our story of Jesus meeting the woman at the well, it is interesting that Jesus is resting in that scene. Weary from traveling, Jesus sends his disciples into town for food while He takes some time to relax and rest, just to put His feet up. I don't know about you, but I don't always have the common sense to do that. If I'm tired, sometimes I just keep going and going, hoping I can outrun my weariness.

Why do we keep running when we are weary? Sometimes we run because we don't know how to stop, caught up in an activist, performance-oriented culture that compels us to do, do, do instead of just to be. Like a toy wound too tightly, we just keep spinning and spinning at times dangerously out of control. We don't know how to stop . . . or we may be afraid to stop. Ceasing the outer activities of our lives compels us to look within ourselves and that can be unsettling.

I remember a phone call I received one Christmas. I was caught up in the rush of the holiday season feeling exactly like that wound-up toy: frantic, spinning. The call was from a friend of mine who was in the throes of a divorce. The franticness I felt was nothing compared to Barry's desperation as he tried to keep his life on an even keel in the midst of so much uncertainty. An outgoing, active person, Barry discovered that living in an empty apartment after being surrounded by a wife and kids was excruciatingly lonely. To escape the loneliness, he found himself frequenting bars, driving his car too fast, drinking more than he should.

I had agreed to talk with Barry on the phone periodically to offer accountability and support. As I listened to him describe his life, it sounded as if his drivenness was luring him away from that quiet center he had once known. Yes, he agreed. He wanted to get back to that quiet center. But how?

I sensed that Barry needed to enter into a "prayer of rest," as Richard Foster calls it. "When all around us is chaos and confusion, deep within we know stability and serenity," Foster writes about this kind of prayer.[2] Such serenity is not something we can manufacture on our own. It is a gift.

In prayer, Barry and I asked for that gift. It is Jesus who gives us rest (Matthew 11:28). I knew in order for Barry to experience the deep rest he needed, he would have to draw close to Jesus. It seemed the best place to do this was a place that Barry found naturally restful.

I asked Barry to picture a tranquil place in his memory. He had no trouble doing this. He immediately recalled a peaceful place he used to frequent as a boy. Barry hadn't thought of this wonderful spot for years, but in prayer it all came back.

He described walking under a tunnel of trees on a warm summer day along a path that led to his favorite swimming hole. I asked if he could imagine Jesus there too. "Yes," said Barry, "He's walking beside me like a friend. He wants to hear everything I have to say." Barry was moved by how much Jesus cared about him.

Like a child eager to share a secret with a friend, Barry ran ahead, anxious to show Jesus his swimming hole. Barry described a cool stream that broadened out into a shady, rock-sheltered pool by a green meadow. "It looks so inviting on a hot day," he said, "you just want to jump in."

So that's what Barry did in his mind's eye. Then he pictured himself lying lazily on the grass after a cool swim. "You don't have to dry off with a towel," he explained, "you just let the water drip off your chest and let it evaporate." Even over the phone, I could tell by the soothing tone of his voice that Barry felt completely relaxed as he imagined himself as a boy again, soaking up the sunshine.

Barry pictured Jesus sitting close beside him on a rock. I asked if Barry heard Jesus say anything to him. We waited in silence. Then Barry said softly, "He knows what I'm going through . . . there are no easy answers."

Then as the scene unfolded, we saw Jesus lean down and lay His hand on Barry's as if to impress deeply on him that He shared in Barry's suffering. Barry could feel the scars and nailprint in the palm of Jesus' hand. Then Jesus interlocked His fingers around Barry's almost in a wrestling hold. We thought of Jesus' hands wrestling in prayer in the Garden of Gethsamane; Jacob wrestling with an angel. Jesus seemed to be intimating that Barry shouldn't run away from the wrestling of this hard time, but that he should engage it, deepening his relationship with God and himself. Jesus assured Barry that He would be there for him in the thick of that struggle as a Friend, offering support and strength.

At that point Barry became utterly vulnerable. In prayer, he turned to Jesus and buried his head in His shoulder, sobbing like a child. "I'm afraid," Barry whispered. "I'm so afraid." For a long few moments, Barry rested in the arms of Jesus, letting go of his fear and worry about the future. "Let go of those heavy concerns," Jesus seemed to say, "and rest here with me." Barry did that, and I suggested that he continue to picture himself resting in the arms of Jesus as he drifted off to sleep that night. In this way, Jesus was able to fill the aching void in Barry's life with His love and comfort. Barry woke up the next morning truly rested.

What surprised me was the way I felt the next morning. I felt more rested and refreshed than I had been for months! The franticness I had been caught up in was simply gone. Coming into the presence of Jesus with Barry, though I was not the one being ministered to, filled me too with an inexplicable peace, and gave me a quiet centeredness even in the midst of my stressful life.

In prayer, we really can stop the world and get off. Be still. Relax. Regain our inner equilibrium. Let Jesus come close and heal a heartache, enter His rest and be refreshed in His love.

THE GIFT OF REFRESHMENT: PURITY

Water is restful. Think of that well-known image in Psalm 23 of the Good Shepherd leading His sheep beside "still waters" to restore their souls. In Isaiah the Lord promises, "I will extend peace to her like a river" and in Revelation, a picture is given of heaven with a "pure river of water of life" flowing from God's throne. This crystal-clear river nourishes lush fruit trees whose leaves are for the "healing of the nations" (Revelation 22:2).

God's refreshment is for healing as well as for rest. We've

shown how God can pour "living water" into a troubled heart through prayer to infuse healing and wholeness. Another healing quality of the living water is its purity.

In this day and age of polluted rivers and oceans stained with oil slicks, it is hard for us to imagine *pure* water. As human beings living in a fallen, sullied world, even contemplating the idea of a crystal-clear river flowing from heaven sounds foreign, faraway. Unobtainable. And yet we were created as good and beautiful, in the image of a holy, loving God, and so it is natural to have an inborn longing for such purity. However, knowing how far short we fall of that goodness, we often feel unworthy and debased.

This was the Samaritan woman's problem. If you remember in the story, the woman draws back when Jesus asks her for a drink because Jesus is a Jew and she is a Samaritan. Samaritans were so despised by Jews that a Jew was considered "unclean" if he even used a drinking vessel handled by a Samaritan. "How can He imagine contaminating Himself by asking *me* for a drink!" she thinks.

But the woman soon learns that Jesus is not bound by prejudice: He is open and accepting of everyone. Nor does He push her away in righteous judgment when He reveals that He knows she has had five husbands and isn't married to the man she is living with now. He sees her future, not her failure; her potential, not her past. Yes, her life is tainted, but Jesus did not come to purify what was already clean, or to heal those who were already well (Matthew 9:12).

Like the Samaritan woman, we often draw back from God's grace because we feel "unclean." Yet that's exactly what the "living water" is for—to cleanse us from the dirt of sin, shame, and guilt.

"I knew Jesus as a child and felt his love," said Sandy, a modern Samaritan woman, "but as I grew older and took the wrong path in life, I felt dirty and unloved, unworthy of God's love. I didn't think He could ever love me again."

Sandy attended the retreat by the beautiful lake which I mentioned earlier. As I described the immense love that God has for us, she began to realize that she had looked for love in all the wrong places: shallow relationships, alcohol, material possessions. None of it satisfied. In corporate prayer, I asked each woman at the retreat to imagine herself as the Samaritan woman meeting Jesus at the well. Sandy told me later that she had no trouble doing this. She felt just like that woman! She knew how heavy the woman's burden was, she knew her shame and when she looked into Jesus' eyes, she saw the same forgiveness and compassion. Sandy accepted the free gift of His love in that moment. And for the first time in her life, she felt forgiven, clean.

Even though it was an inner-healing retreat, I asked people to come forward after the talk if they wanted to accept Jesus that night as Savior and Lord (accepting Jesus into our hearts is the greatest inner healing any of us can experience). Sandy came forward. With tears of joy streaming down her face, she said, "I've finally found what I've been looking for all my life."

Like David, the cry of Sandy's heart was: "Lord, create in me a clean heart" (Psalm 51:10). And He did. As Sandy emptied her heart of wrong desires and feelings of unworthiness, Jesus was free to fill the cup of her heart with His purity and His acceptance. "Repent, then, and turn to God, so that your sins may be wiped out, that times of refreshing may come from the Lord" (Acts 3:19 NIV). "And everyone who has this hope in Him purifies Himself, just as He is pure" (1 John 3:3).

How refreshing can God's cleansing be? "Wash me thoroughly," David prayed. "Cleanse me with hyssop . . . wash me and I will be whiter than snow" (Psalm 52:7 NIV). Think of feeling squeaky clean after taking a long, cool shower; or breathing in the sweet, minty scent of hyssop; or looking with amazement at the purity of newly fallen snow.

Can God really clean up the "oil spills" of our lives and restore the pristine quality of who we were meant to be? Yes. He does it not only once—in that glorious moment when we first come to know His saving grace—but again and again. "If we confess our sins, He is faithful and just to forgive us our sins and to cleanse us from all unrighteousness" (1 John 1:9).

A word of caution: at times even after we have received God's forgiveness, we still *feel* condemned. What we feel is not God's lack of forgiveness, but our own. "Do not call anything impure that God has made clean" (Acts 10:15 NIV). Even though we disparage ourselves, the Holy Spirit is ever-present within us to help cleanse us even of this self-punishing attitude. As we are filled more and more with the Spirit, we not only experience His kindness and gentleness toward others, but also toward ourselves (Galatians 5:22, 23). This too is a gift.

Once the cup of our heart is empty and cleansed and filled with His holiness, Jesus lavishly pours in the sparkling gift of His joy.

THE GIFT OF REFRESHMENT: JOY

"Therefore with joy you will draw water from the wells of salvation" (Isaiah 12:3). I believe that joy—the effervescent, unseen quality of Jesus' love—was also a part of the refreshment the Samaritan woman received at the well of Sychar that day.

Remember the story again. What do we see? We see the woman take time out from her busy chores to enter into a dialogue with Jesus. We see her rest. We can even see her draw close to Jesus as she drinks in His acceptance and she begins to accept herself. We see her purified. But joy? That's left to our imaginations.

We know that the woman came burdened to the well, carrying a heavy earthen jar. But when she returns to the village, she leaves the jar behind. We know that she came out to the well alone to avoid the villagers, yet after being with Jesus, she goes back to the village telling everyone about the Man who touched her in such a way that she wants everyone else to know Him too. There must have been something about the way she looked, the sense of urgency in her voice, that convinced them because they all went out to meet Jesus, and Scripture tells us, "Many of the Samaritans of that city believed in Him because of the word of the woman" (John 4:39).

I wonder. Did she walk back to the village to share her exciting news, or did she run? Did her face shine as Moses' did when he met God face to face (Exodus 34:29)? Why did she leave her jar behind? Didn't work matter anymore? And suddenly this woman who was ashamed to show her face now urges others to follow her—and they listen! There must have been a new vibrance and boldness in her that they found compelling. This, to me, speaks of joy.

What does this kind of joy look like? I asked the Lord this question in prayer one morning when I was at a winter retreat center surrounded by snow-covered pines. As I looked out the window early in the morning, I saw a shower of tiny snow crystals, barely visible, glimmering in the sunshine. And I knew that those "sparkles in the air" somehow captured the elusive, but unmistakeable feeling that dances in the hearts of those who come fully alive in Christ as the Samaritan woman did that day.

It is a joy we all can experience as we draw close to Jesus and let Him refresh us in His love. We can experience it in brief moments, like a glimpse out the window on a winter morning; we can experience it in a worship celebration; we can experience it in hushed moments of prayer; we can experience it in the encouragement of a friend. But there is nowhere that we taste it more intimately and personally than when we dip into the well of Scripture.

As the Samaritan woman came close to Jesus and drank His love deeply into her spirit, letting it refresh and enliven her, so we can drink in His love too by allowing the words of Scripture to water the wasteland of our hearts. "If you drink the water that I give you _____ (insert your name), you will never thirst. But the water I give you will become in you a fountain of water springing up into everlasting life" (John 4:14).

We need to learn to "drink in" God's Word, to let it infuse our inner being. To illustrate this at retreats, I ask everyone to suck on a peppermint candy while they hear the passage of the woman at the well read out loud. "How sweet are Your words to my taste!" exclaimed the Psalmist (Psalm 119:103). Tasting the mint—sweet, refreshing, clean, cool—allows the listeners to literally savor each word and phrase as it is spoken.

Try that right now. Take time to relax and really listen to God's love expressed to *you* in Scripture.[3] Taste and savor the freshness of each word. These verses are personalized to help you do that:

> For I will comfort you,
> I will comfort all your waste places;
> I will make your wilderness like Eden,
> And your desert like the garden of the
>   Lord;
> Joy and gladness will be found in it,

Thanksgiving and the voice of melody.
                                    —Isaiah 51:3

And the desert shall rejoice and
    blossom as the rose;
It shall blossom abundantly and rejoice . . .
                                    —Isaiah 35:1–2

For you are greatly beloved . . .
                                    —Daniel 9:23

Yes, I have loved you with an everlasting love;
Therefore with lovingkindness I have drawn you.
                                    —Jeremiah 31:3

How precious is Your lovingkindness, O
    God! . . .
[I am] abundantly satisfied with the fullness
    of Your house,
And You give [me] drink from the
    river of Your pleasures.
For with You is the fountain of life . . .
                                    —Psalm 36:7–9

Can you hear the Lord of Love wooing you with these words? Can you sense His delight in you? His pleasure? Can you picture yourself as a well-watered garden? A rose suddenly blooming in a desert?

That's how Jesus sees you. He sees possibilities in you that you aren't even aware of. He sees your promise, your giftedness, your infinite worth. That is what He saw in the woman at the well, and it transformed her. She came into Jesus' presence weary from hurt and went away energized by healing; she came thirsty and left fulfilled. He can do the same for you and me.

ARE YOU THIRSTY?

"Come! Whoever is thirsty, come, take the free gift of the water of life" (Revelation 22:17). Are you thirsty? Perhaps like my friend Barry, you are weary from running: either tired of running from yourself or just tired of trying to do too much. You need an oasis of rest. *Come,* says Jesus.

Perhaps like Sandy, our modern Samaritan woman, you feel dirty and unloved. You have looked for love in all the wrong places. Nothing satisfies. You want what Jesus has to offer, but you still feel unworthy of His love. *Come,* says Jesus.

Perhaps you have a personal relationship with Christ, but you have not been close to Him for a while. You have lost your "drinkable" spirit. You have devotional times, but they are rushed and superficial. Take time now to drink deeply of His presence. *Come,* says Jesus.

Come.

THE GIFT
OF REFRESHMENT

 ead and Reflect on John 4:5–14

So He (Jesus) came to a city of Samaria which is called Sychar, near the plot of ground that Jacob gave to his son Joseph. Now Jacob's well was there. Jesus therefore, being wearied from His journey, sat thus by the well. It was about the sixth hour.

A woman of Samaria came to draw water. Jesus said to her, "Give Me a drink . . ."

Then the woman of Samaria said to Him, "How is it that You, being a Jew, ask a drink from me, a Samaritan woman?" For Jews have no dealings with Samaritans.

Jesus answered and said to her, "If you knew the gift of God, and who it is who says to you, 'Give Me a drink,' you would have asked Him, and He would have given you living water."

The woman said to Him, "Sir, You have nothing to draw with, and the well is deep. Where then do You get that living water? Are You greater than our father Jacob, who gave us the well, and drank from it himself, as well as his sons and his livestock?"

Jesus answered and said to her, "Whoever drinks of this water will thirst again, but whoever drinks of the water that I shall give him will never thirst. But the water that I shall give him will become in him a fountain of water springing up into everlasting life."

The woman said to Him, "Sir, give me this water that I may not thirst, nor come here to draw."

Can you picture yourself as the Samaritan woman coming to draw water from the well?

It's noon. The sun high overhead is oppressive. You are tired, hot. Your feet shuffle along a dry, dusty path, a path that you have walked hundreds of times . . . out to the well, back again, out to the well, back again, out to the well . . . Feel the jar on your shoulder. It's *so* heavy. What's in the jar? Are there responsibilities, worries that weigh you down? Take a moment to imagine what these might be.

In the distance you see the well. You hesitate. Someone is sitting there. You don't want to meet anybody at the well today. Most of the women in the village come to the well in the cool of the evening. You're coming now to avoid them. The other women know what your life is like. They talk about you behind your back and look at you in that hard way that hurts.

Reluctantly, you decide to go on toward the well, determined to get your water quickly and leave. As you draw close to the well, though, you're surprised. You see a man sitting there. A stranger, someone you've never seen before. Your eyes meet His . . . His eyes are not like the others. They are kind. Compassionate.

He invites you to sit down on the well beside Him and rest. Rest? You still have so much to do today. Can you spare the time? Slowly, you put aside your jar. Yes. Maybe you will take a moment just to rest and relax. If there is something you need to put aside, but can't, let Jesus help you. Picture what He might do.

Then see Him smile and ask you for a drink. "Why would He ask *me* for a drink?" you wonder. He's a Jew and you're a Samaritan. . . . He's holy and you feel so unworthy.

Do you hold back from Jesus because you feel unclean? If so, confess any sin and let Him cleanse you completely, then fill you up with His love (1 John 1:9).

"If you knew who asked you for a drink," Jesus says. "If you really knew Me, I would give you a gift. A gift of living water."

Is it hard for you to accept gifts? Perhaps you are a giver who has difficulty receiving. Intellectually, you know grace is a gift, but secretly you still believe that your relationship with Jesus is something you need to work at or even earn. If so, ask Him to show you why you are this way. Give Him your performance-orientation, your need to control, whatever it is that you need to let go of in order to receive freely. Then let Him give you Himself.

Suddenly you realize that *He* is the living water. Jesus is the giver and the gift. All that He asks for is the empty cup of your heart and He will fill it with *His* rest, *His* cleansing, *His* joy. As you open your heart to Him,

> He fills it,
> and fills it,
> and fills it . . .
> to overflowing.

After being in the presence of Jesus, you feel rejuvenated, brand new. You run back to the village exhilarated—with a secret to share, not to hide. There are so many who are needy like you. Even the women who look at you with scorn; they seem so bitter, so unhappy. They need the living water too. But for now, until the time comes to share it, it is a shimmering secret meant just for you.

THE GIFT
OF EMPOWERMENT

"Freely you have received, freely give."
—*Matthew 10:8*

*A*t the beginning of this book, I told a story about a mother who suddenly lost her son in a tragic accident. In her grief, she opened herself to God in prayer and received healing in ways she never thought possible. What she experienced was a healing moment, something she came to think of as a "bright gift." Searching for words to describe this moving experience, she said, "it was like a river of love that flowed out to me, through me, and out to the rest of the world."

Love flowed in . . . and love flowed out. She discovered that the healing moment was not only a gift to receive, but also to give away. As she let God's healing transform her from within, she became, very naturally, without any effort of her own, a more giving person. She reached out to others in compassion— learning to hug, learning to listen, learning to comfort as she had been comforted. Freely she had received, and freely she began to give.

In this last chapter, we're going to focus on how God empowers us to help others, how we can become "gifted givers." Do you recall Henri Nouwen's quote from the first chapter? "We are all healers who can reach out to offer health, and patients in constant need of health." This statement may sound challenging, or frightening. You may wonder how you could ever be instrumental in someone else's healing. Perhaps you feel inadequate, ill-equipped, or feel you don't have enough faith . . . and, of course, you still have problems of your own.

It's important to remember that we are people in process. There may be certain areas of our lives where we've received significant healing. At the same time, we still know how needy we are in other areas. God can use our strengths, or He may choose to use our weaknesses, sometimes with even greater effect. When Paul complained about his weaknesses to God, God answered, "My grace is sufficient for you, for My strength is made perfect in weakness" (2 Corinthians 12:9). It is often in those areas where we feel most inadequate that we are most "usable" because we are relying on God's strength, not our own.

We are strong and we are weak; we have been healed, and yet we are broken. God asks us to reach out to a broken world, in the midst of our own brokenness. To begin right where we are.

I'd like to encourage you now to think of yourself not only as a "patient," aware of your own needs, but also as a "healer," someone who has much to give others.

BECOMING A GIFTED GIVER

"When I was still a new widow," a friend told me, "I drank in every hug I received. I could always count on one particular woman to give me a warm greeting and hug on Sunday morning. On one of those mornings, I remember thanking the Lord for that hug especially needed that day. Jesus' reply was, *She is My arms to you. Now you be My arms to others.*

Think of the ways people have reached out to you when you were hurting. Perhaps someone gave *you* a hug at a time when you felt unloved. Perhaps you received a note of encouragement when you were struggling with despair. Maybe a friend was there just when you needed someone to talk to, to help shoulder a burden that was too heavy to bear alone. Is there any reason you can't do that for someone else?

Jesus uses our arms, our words, our ears to express His love and healing. Each of us is uniquely suited to do this in different ways. We were even created with that in mind. "For we are His workmanship, created in Christ Jesus for good works, which God prepared beforehand that we should walk in them" (Ephesians 2:10).

You are a gifted person. You have skills and abilities, talents, resources that can be put to use right away to bring healing to others. In addition to these tangible resources, you also have intangible resources at your disposal: the kind of person you are, your unique personality and temperament traits. Finally, you may not think of your own brokenness as a gift, but it can be: it is often your richest resource in reaching out to someone in need. How can these resources be used for healing? Let me give you some examples.

Sharing your skills and talents. I have a friend who is a business consultant. He uses his professional skills to help ex-prisoners find employment through a company he's set up specifically for this purpose. Even though he's a successful businessman, Tom came from a dysfunctional family himself and can identify with the low self-worth that many inmates feel. Tom's own brokenness has given him an incredible compassion for hurting men. As well as the financial assistance Tom gives these men to help them rebuild their lives, he spends long hours listening to their pain, offering support and encouragement.

I have another friend who has been a social worker much of her life and is sensitive to the needs of children from broken homes. She heads up a *Moms-In-Touch* prayer group of neighbors who pray for students and teachers at their local school. Nancy is also a foster mom who uses her nurturing skills to hold and bless little ones as Jesus would, providing a foundation of love for the rest of their lives.

Sharing your resources. Jody has a "friendship healing" ministry. Her greatest resource is her home and a warm, affectionate family. Knowing that loneliness is a great source of hurt in our society, Jody invites single parents, neglected teenagers and others on their own to share in family dinners. If she takes her family to a volleyball game or potluck, she'll invite a neighbor, perhaps a new divorcee, who may feel excluded by other family and friends. "I'm constantly amazed," she says, "how much people appreciate a small invitation. 'Thanks for including me,' they say again and again."

Sharing who you are. God uses not only our natural skills and abilities and resources—what we *do* in life—to bring healing, but also who we *are*. You may have an outgoing personality and find it easy to express affection openly. Your natural gifts can go a long way to give the gift of healing to others. A smile can uplift a sagging spirit; a loving embrace can soothe the hurt of rejection.

On the other hand, you may be a shy, reticent person. I have a friend who finds it hard to hug. Even though she has been healed of much abuse in her background, she still is uncomfortable expressing affection openly. So she sends "hugs" through the mail. A gifted and sensitive writer, Maya's words of comfort minister to many. She often enhances her own words by including a verse from Scripture. The Word of God dropped into someone's life during a time of need has tremendous power to heal as the psalmist testifies, "He sent His word and healed them" (Psalm 107:20).

Sharing your story. In addition to using our skills and abilities and who we are, God can use the most basic stuff of our lives to minister to others: our stories. Everyone has a story. Hearing about how God works in ordinary people's lives is riveting and often moves us much more than a sermon preached from a pulpit.

Tom, the man I mentioned earlier who ministers in prisons, took his friend Wayne along one night to a Christian fellowship group at a high security prison. "You know, I don't know why I'm going with you," Wayne confided to Tom, beginning to get cold feet. "I don't really feel I belong here."

Wayne felt awkward at first sitting around a table with convicted criminals, but as everyone began to share their hurts and needs, the Holy Spirit brought a tender vulnerability. The sharing went deeper. Wayne revealed a source of hurt in his own life: his son's chemical dependency, which had brought great destruction, nearly ruining his son's life and his own. Wayne broke down in tears remembering the pain. There was a long silence. Then a young prisoner, in tears too, turned to Wayne and told him how much his story meant to him. As he heard it, it was as if a light had gone on in his head, allowing him to see the depth of hurt he had caused his own parents and himself by his drug abuse.

Recalling that stirring moment, Tom said, "It was as if all heaven and earth were moving in that room as that young prisoner's heart changed."

As Tom and Wayne drove home that night from the prison, Wayne smiled. "Now I know why I had to come tonight."

MOVING INTO MINISTRY

By now you have no trouble recognizing that the unusual experience in the prison that night was a healing moment. But it is hard to say whether the young prisoner was more deeply touched or Wayne. Wayne might have discovered for the first time that night the joy of ministry. Called out of his comfort zone to respond to the needs of others, Wayne had to reach beyond his natural skills and talents and rely on something more: the Holy Spirit. In partnership with the Holy Spirit, Wayne did something he never could have done on his own and it was exciting.

As we begin to use our natural gifts to serve others in Jesus' name, we discover new capabilities that are not natural to us at all. These capabilities, borne of the Spirit, are called spiritual gifts. The Greek word for "spiritual gift" is *charismata*, which means "a gift of God's grace." Spiritual gifts, bestowed by God and empowered by the Holy Spirit, are given to us specifically to do God's work.

Spiritual gifts are supernatural, not natural, but they may build on our natural gifts. Or they may not be connected at all. For example, Wayne might have had a natural ability to share his feelings with other people, but in the context of that Spirit-filled moment, God might have given him a new freedom to share his heart with greater depth than he ever had before and to know exactly what to share—those things specifically that the young prisoner needed to hear.

On the other hand, Wayne might have been a naturally reserved person and talking openly about his feelings as he did that night might have astonished him. If this were the case, Wayne would be the first one to tell you that the words that came out of his mouth had to be from the Holy Spirit because they certainly weren't from him! That experience might have birthed something new as the Holy Spirit transformed Wayne's natural reserve into supernatural boldness as he stepped out to share his faith, something that could be possible through the spiritual gifts of healing or teaching or evangelism.

Everyone in the Body of Christ has one or more spiritual gifts (1 Corinthians 12:7). These special capabilities are given as gifts, but we are responsible for developing them. Just as you have to develop a natural gift, e.g., playing an instrument if you are gifted in music, you develop your spiritual gifts by using them—finding out if you enjoy them, if you can use them effectively, and if others in the Body of Christ confirm this as well.

Do you know what your spiritual gifts are? Scripture says that we should, "*eagerly desire* spiritual gifts" (1 Corinthians 14:1 NIV, italics added). If you are a man or woman who is sensitive to the needs of people around you, and you know the power of God to help, then you should be about the task of discovering and developing your spiritual gifts so that you can be better equipped to meet those needs.

DEVELOPING HEALING GIFTS

As I have said, all of us can use our natural and spiritual gifts to bring healing to others. Just as all Christians are expected to share their faith, even though they don't have the specific gift of evangelism, I believe all Christians can pray for healing. I have tried to suggest throughout this book ways in which you can do this within the ordinary context of everyday living.

If your child is sick, you will naturally pray for your son or daughter to get well. In addition to the normal way you might pray, try some of the suggestions I described in chapter four, e.g., laying a hand on a feverish forehead as you pray or using words of Scripture along with your own words to picture health instead of sickness. If a neighbor or officemate shares an emotional hurt, remember the tools of inner-healing prayer: listening with love, affirmation, caring touch.

We can all do these things. But above and beyond that, some people do have a "calling" to exercise and grow in specific gifts of healing. How do you know if you have healing gifts? I'm sure everybody's story is different, but I discovered my calling first through a natural interest. As I shared in chapter four, my interest was sparked when a group of friends challenged me to ask, "What does the Bible say about healing? Does God heal today?" As we put into practice what we learned, it became more compelling. I felt a heart tug toward this ministry.

This heart tug came in two ways. On the one hand, I developed a piercing awareness of the pain in people's lives, often "hidden" pain that others couldn't see. At the same time, I drew closer to God's heart than I ever had before as my prayer life intensified. God is love: to draw close to His heart of compassion is to begin to feel what He feels. I began to share *His* grief when I saw men and women hurting; *His* longing to wipe away tears; *His* yearning to mend the broken pieces of their lives.

At times, the grief became almost too great. For a long time, I saw hurt and I knew God's desire to heal, but I couldn't connect the two. I wanted God to use me to bring healing to others, but I didn't how to do it. Again and again, I heard the same message in prayer that the disciples had heard when Jesus commissioned them to go out in His name: "I'm going to send you what my Father has promised, but stay in the city until you

have been clothed with power from on high" (Luke 24:4
Wait. Be patient. You will be empowered.

God kept his promise to me as He did to the disciple
gift of empowerment did come. It slowly unfolded as I
the Word and prayer every day; as I diligently learned all
could about the subject through books, tapes, and seminars; as
gifted men and women came into my life to help point the way;
as God healed the brokenness in my own life; and as I began to
ask, "What am I uniquely called to do?"

As Walter Wink says, "We are not called to do everything,
to heal everything, to change everything, but only to do what
God asks of us. And in the asking is supplied the power to
perform it."[1]

God asks; we answer. The call to healing begins with a compelling awareness of human hurt. Something in you suddenly
"hears" hearts desperately crying out for God's healing. The
Lord of Love asks, *Who will go to love and comfort and dry
a tear?* And much to your surprise, you answer, "Here I am.
Send me."

HERE WE ARE: SEND US

We tend to forget that when we answer God's call to serve
Him we are not alone. We are surrounded by a fellowship of
faith, an enthusiastic community of men and women who are
growing in their gifts too, who are empowered by the Spirit and
are just as much in love with Jesus as we are. God in His sover-
eignty has given each of us different natural gifts and spiritual
gifts so that we are only operating in full power when we are
functioning together as His Body, the church.

Paul likens Christians in the Body of Christ to the different
parts of a human body. "But now indeed there are many mem-

ers, yet one body. And the eye cannot say to the hand, 'I have no need of you'; nor again the head to the feet, 'I have no need of you' (1 Corinthians 12:20–21). Just as in the human body, all members are necessary, so in the Body of Christ every member is necessary and valuable to the working of the whole.

Working together with other members in the Body of Christ provides empowerment too. It is in the context of the Body that we learn what our gifts are and how they can best be used. The church provides a "safe place" where we can risk trying out our new capabilities and receive helpful feedback, mutual support and encouragement, and begin to understand how our specific gifts can best work in concert with others to accomplish God's purposes.

More and more churches are establishing "healing teams" to train and mobilize their members to pray for others. Being part of a healing team is an excellent way to explore an interest in healing and grow in this ministry if it attracts you. Typically, a church will have several weeks of training, describing the biblical basis for healing and prayer methods used, followed by "hands-on" practice. Those who want to go on become part of an organized prayer ministry. Healing teams, usually made up of two to four members, then begin to pray for individuals as they come forward with various needs.

Praying on a team is very exciting. "Now there are diversities of gifts," says Paul, "but the same Spirit" (1 Corinthians 12:4). To watch several healing team members minister together, combining their different gifts and insights, is to see how remarkably this principle works.

For example, let's say a young man comes forward for prayer and is emotionally distraught. He is hurting, but he doesn't know why. As he describes his pain, someone on the team, through the gift of discernment, knows that his root problem is rejection. Another team member senses that inner healing of a past memory would help release this pain. But which memory does Jesus want to touch? Through the gift of knowledge (an insight given by the Spirit to help direct the path of healing), someone else pinpoints a hurtful memory. As prayer delves deeper, an area of hidden hardness reveals a spirit of anger and hatred in the young man's heart that needs to be cast out. A deliverance prayer is offered. In this way, ministry progresses step by step. Like the beautiful blend of different instruments in an orchestra, the Holy Spirit orchestrates every gift, every insight to a single end: healing.

This process may sound complicated and lengthy, but it isn't. The prayer time I've just described might take twenty to thirty minutes. It might take a therapist or counselor years to achieve what was achieved in that short time. Team ministry multiplies the efficiency and effectiveness of prayer and provides a breadth of empowerment we could never achieve on our own.

In addition to becoming involved in team ministry, another way to grow in the healing gifts is to find a prayer partner, someone like yourself who has a heart of compassion and wants to learn how to pray for others. I have several prayer partners. One of my prayer partners is also my mentor. She is further along in the healing ministry than I am and I learn from her as I support her in prayer. I have other prayer partners who are learning from me as they support me in prayer. Learning to pray and minister to others is a constant call to climb higher in the Spirit. "I press on toward the goal for the prize of the upward call of God in Christ Jesus," said Paul (Philippians 3:14 RSV). So together we press on.

Climbing higher in the Spirit, like scaling a mountain, can be exhilarating, a wonderful adventure. But like any kind of adventure, it has its hazards too.

VOCATIONAL HAZARDS

It is hard to write about hazards in the healing ministry because they are "dangers of the heart," and our hearts are such an amalgam of mixed motives, desires and needs. Each of us has different human weaknesses, unhealed areas in our lives that make us vulnerable as we reach out to help others. This is why it is critical that anyone called into this ministry is mindful of his or her own woundedness. A word of caution about four potential dangers:

Healing hurts. Compassionate people are drawn into the healing ministry with their hearts wide open ready to help. And pain floods in. It can be overwhelming. It is easy to forget that the hands we open to others in prayer are not our own but Jesus' hands. Even though we know that we cannot and should not take the pain of others into our own hearts, we do. Becoming overburdened can lead to burnout.

I asked an experienced friend how she avoids becoming overwhelmed by the pain dropped into her hands. When she feels overloaded, she says, she knows she has to give the pain back to Jesus. She does this literally by holding a small wooden cross in her hand and emotionally letting the pain drain out of her and into the cross, where it belongs. I have found this a great help too. Jesus said that "His burden is light," and it is when we only bear our part.

Ministry is seductive. It is deeply satisfying to meet people's needs. If you discover that your true calling in life is healing prayer, you will enjoy it immensely. To see burdens lifted through prayer, tears turn to joy, captives set free will even give you a "spiritual high." It's so breathtaking, you'll want to do it all the time! And of course we all know how great the need is.

However, our hearts can run away with us. We can be so busy

meeting other people's needs that we forget the needs of our families, our friends, our primary responsibilities. This is particularly a problem for natural caretakers who often serve others out of a need to be needed. The solution? Accountability from others, self-awareness, and a disciplined prayer life that lets the Holy Spirit convict us of "unholy" tendencies.

The Messianic complex. I remember hearing Keith Miller confess that he took himself off the lecture circuit for two years because people were so adoring and had such wonderful things to say about his abilities that he began to believe it himself! This is an easy trap for people in the healing ministry to fall into too.

We do not heal. Jesus does. It is easy for spiritual power to become intertwined with personal power: when this happens, pride comes into play. To curb this tendency, it is helpful to share leadership responsibilities with others, say no to tempting ministry opportunities sometimes, and humble yourself before the Lord in the Word and prayer.

Spiritual warfare. To pray for healing, as loving and good as it is, is to step foot on a battlefield. When we enter the arena of prayer, we become engaged in spiritual warfare, the constant battle being waged between the unseen powers of good and evil, darkness and light (Ephesians 6:12). Just as a soldier would not step onto a real battlefield without protection, a healing minister must also be protected.

We can pray for spiritual protection daily by putting on the full armor of God (Ephesians 6:1–18), a way to ready ourselves to stand in Jesus' strength, not our own.[2] In addition to praying for our own protection, healing ministers need to ask others to pray for their protection too, which is why it is so important to have prayer partners.

These dangers may seem daunting, but they simply underscore our need for absolute dependence upon Jesus. "Without me," Jesus said, "you can do nothing" (John 15:5). The more the Spirit empowers us, the more we realize how powerless we are on our own. And that takes us to the foot of the cross.

THE WAY OF THE CROSS

"When we pick up the cross of Jesus and bear it in love to Him, His Kingdom has begun in us," writes Francois Fenelon, a seventeenth-century priest.[3] When I picked up the cross of Jesus years ago to help others find healing, I never could have guessed where that journey would take me. I am not the same person I was then. I will not be the same person tomorrow. Jesus is changing me, little by little, moment by moment, as I give Him more and more freedom to be Lord of my life.

"Penetrate and possess my whole being so utterly that all my life may only be a radiance of yours," prayed Cardinal Newman. "The light, oh Lord, will be all from you; none of it will be mine; it will be you shining on others through me."[4]

This is a daring prayer. This is the prayer of the gifted giver, fully surrendered, fully released, fully abandoned to the will of God. It is not a prayer that is answered easily or quickly; it is rather the prayer of a lifetime. Becoming a gifted giver involves more than extending compassion to another, or offering the gift of prayer. It involves giving *yourself* away. "I have been crucified with Christ," wrote Paul, "it is no longer I who live, but Christ lives in me," (Galatians 2:20).

As much as I love the healing ministry, I would be less than honest if I did not say that there are times when bearing the cross of Christ becomes too heavy, too hard. When that happens, just when I am facing my own limitations and inadequacies, I am sent a word of encouragement. It might be a word of Scripture, a friend's affirmation, the words of a song, the tender presence of the Holy Spirit.

One of these moments of encouragement came while I sat in church one Sunday. During a Lenten service, my pastor, Arthur Rouner, preached on "The Way of the Cross."[5] When we begin to identify with Jesus and pick up His cross, he said, we see the world from a different perspective.

"It never looks the same again. The world always has a different color, a different cast, a different hue, a different meaning, once you see it from the vantage point of the cross of Christ.

"It's a world of pain," he continued. "It's a vale of tears. It is a world of injustice. And you—you are the King's man, the King's woman. And you're stuck. You can't ignore it. You have to love it. Because the cross is about ransom. The cross is about a price paid. The cross is about buying back all the dark and doubt and death of the devil—and giving the world a new start."

Yes! I agreed with Arthur. That's what I want my ministry to do—give the world a new start. There can be no higher calling, no greater joy than helping others find healing and hope. But I was finding that as I grew in my gifts and dared to risk more in prayer, that the Lord entrusted me with more difficult assignments—the situations I was led to pray for were increasingly more painful, more complex, more arduous. I felt more like a flimsy sapling being blown about by the wind than the strong and sturdy oak that I wanted to be.

As I listened to Arthur's words that morning, though, I began to feel an inner strengthening. Behind Arthur and above him as he preaches from the pulpit is a plain wooden cross. As he preached that morning about standing in the cross with Jesus, I felt I was literally placed in the middle of that cross and I had a sensation of tree roots beneath me shooting down deep into the ground rooting me there. I heard the words "stand firm."

After the service, Arthur invited the congregation forward for personal prayer. I went forward and asked him to pray for me. I explained what I was feeling—my fearfulness, and yet there was God's call that morning to have courage, not to flinch, to stand firm.

As Arthur prayed for me, I was reminded of Paul's words to his timid disciple Timothy: "fan into flame the gift of God, which is in you through the laying on of my hands" (2 Timothy 1:6 NIV). In the Bible the laying on of hands not only imparts healing, but it also imparts spiritual power. The Holy Spirit flows through one person to another in love and power, strengthening the receiver for service or to take a new step of faith.

Arthur is a veteran pastor of sixty-five, gifted in healing. When he laid hands on me in prayer, his healing touch fanned the flame of God's gifts within me and I felt a new surge of spiritual power, a fresh outpouring of the Holy Spirit. After prayer that morning, I walked away no longer trembling, but solid inside. Instead of fear, I felt resolve; instead of timidity, courage. "For God has not given us a spirit of fear, but of power and of love and of a sound mind" (2 Timothy 1:7). This is the gift of empowerment.

FAN THE FLAME

There are bright gifts of service that burn within you too. You are the King's man, the King's woman gifted to bear the cross of Christ into a hurting world. As you discover the resources of empowerment—your natural gifts, your spiritual gifts, working together with the Body of Christ and being renewed by the Holy Spirit—you will grow as a gifted giver.

Fan into flame the gifts you've been given. And as the healing light of God's love penetrates and possesses you, that inner radiance will touch and heal others.

Let's nourish that inner radiance now through prayer. Come close to Jesus and let Him bless you and send you out in His name. Go forth in gratitude, gladly receiving, gladly giving.

THE GIFT
OF EMPOWERMENT

 ead and Reflect
on Luke 24:49–52

"Behold, I send the Promise of My Father upon you; but tarry in the city of Jerusalem until you are endued with power from on high."

And He led them out as far as Bethany, and He lifted up His hands and blessed them. Now it came to pass, while He blessed them, that He was parted from them and carried up into heaven. And they worshiped Him, and returned to Jerusalem with great joy . . .

Imagine yourself as one of Jesus' disciples. As you walk beside Jesus, you are mindful of His footsteps on the path next to yours. You have walked so many miles together during the last three years. The crowds, the clamor, the excitement of it all fades in a blur; what you remember most are the times you were alone with Jesus. The long, searching conversations around the campfire at night, the sound of His laughter, His friendship . . .

This is the last good-bye. In your heart of hearts, you know He is not coming back. Your heart is heavy. You wish He didn't have to go.

Jesus stops. This is the place, He says. You and your friends gather close in a circle around Him. One by one, He rests His hand on each of you. Now it is your turn. Jesus looks at you with affection. How you love Him. He understands you as no one else ever has, He accepts you as no one else ever could.

Look long at Jesus. Drink in His love for you. Feel His physical presence, the sense of His being there, the substance of who

He is. Let Him touch you and impart a blessing. Feel His glory, His power, His radiance flow into you. "I will empower you," He says softly.

Even as He blesses you, He begins to rise from the ground. You take a step back. Everyone else does too, leaving a little circle of space where He once stood. Slowly, He begins to rise in the air higher and higher.

You feel a stab of panic. You're afraid. You want to live His life out for Him in the world; you want to do what He has asked, but it will be so hard without Him.

He looks down and smiles as if to reassure you. You remember His promise: "I will always be with you."

You can no longer see Jesus. He has risen beyond the clouds. You shake your head as if waking from a dream, still in a daze. After a while, you know it's time to go. You walk back to the city with your friends.

You wonder as you walk. Do you dare believe that the glory that shone in Jesus can shine in you? You feel a longing in your heart, an expectancy. Power will come, said Jesus. Yes, you can already feel a brightness rising within you. Bear it to the world, Jesus seems to intimate with each step, bear My light to the world. You can almost hear His footsteps on the path next to yours . . . and you know, you really know now, that He will always be beside you. Always.

NOTES

❦

Introduction

1. John Wimber and Kevin Springer, *Power Healing* (San Francisco: HarperCollins Publishers, 1987), p. xi.

Chapter 1

1. Francis MacNutt, *The Prayer that Heals* (Notre Dame, IN: Ave Maria Press, 1981), p. 16.

2. Henri Nouwen, *With Open Hands* (Notre Dame, IN: Ave Maria Press, 1972), p. 56.

3. "Guide Me Into an Unclenched Moment" from *Guerillas of Grace* by Ted Loder. © 1984 by Luramedia. Reprinted by permission of Luramedia, Inc., San Diego, California.

4. Henri J. M. Nouwen, *Reaching Out* (Garden City, NY: Doubleday & Company, Inc.), p. 65.

Chapter 2

1. Dennis and Matthew Linn, *Healing Life's Hurts* (New York: Paulist Press, 1978), p. 1.

2. Sandra Wilson's metaphor. Sandra D. Wilson, *Released from Shame* (Downers Grove, IL: InterVarsity Press, 1990), p. 57.

3. Paul Clancy, "Child Sex Abuse: 'Crime of the '90s'" *USA Today,* September 29, 1989, p. A-3.

4. Gail D. Webbe, *The Night and Nothing* (New York: Seabury Press, 1964), p. 109.

5. Henri J. M. Nouwen, *Reaching Out* (Garden City, NY: Doubleday & Company, Inc.), p. 54.

6. Francis MacNutt, *The Prayer That Heals* (Notre Dame, IN: Ave Maria Press, 1981), p. 45.

7. Barbara Shlemon, *Healing the Hidden Self* (Notre Dame, IN: Ave Maria Press, 1982), p. 13.
